OFF TO SEE THE YANKEES

The Baseball Road Trip Guide

STEPHEN J. ROCKWELL • STEVE PIERCE

Copyright © 2017 Stephen J. Rockwell and Steve Pierce.

All rights reserved.

No part of this book may be reproduced in any form or by any means without permission in writing from the authors, except for the inclusion of brief quotations in a review.

Cover Design by Jean-Paul Vest

Bookbaby.com

ISBN: 978-1-48359-740-9

To Ryan, Katie, and Baby Nicole

To Nicole, Rebecca, Owen, and Bailey

Table of Contents

Introduction 1

Baltimore 7

St. Louis 13

Cleveland 19

Minnesota 27

Chicago 37

Kansas City 49

Boston 55

Toronto 65

Tampa, Pittsburgh, and Scranton 77

Miami 85

Introduction

Steve Pierce loves his wife. Nicole is beautiful, smart, and funny. Steve and I both are grateful to her for letting Steve go away on these trips. If not for her willingness to give him a weekend off here and there, we could never make these trips. Steve, in fact, says that these trips have kept his marriage together.

Well, some of that's true. Steve does love his wife, and she is smart, beautiful, and funny. Whether or not these trips have kept his marriage together is a whole other issue. They're happily married, but the trips are probably only part of all that. Nevertheless, the friends of mine who enjoy the happiest marriages understand that both husband and wife need to get away sometimes. Smart wives understand that sports are important, too. But the first bit of advice we'll offer, in starting the discussion about going away for a weekend to see the Yankees, is this: tell your wife you love her.

Even if you don't, of course. The point is to get out of the house.

* * *

Steve and I have been going to one Yankees away series each summer for a lot of years. We've been doing it so long that I'm married, too, now, and I love my wife. She's also beautiful, smart, and funny. (I know, Christine, fourth paragraph, but it's here! Just like I promised!)

Anyway, it occurs to us that these road trips are not a new idea—Yankee fans are everywhere we go, invading away stadiums like happy, arrogant locusts—but there may be folks out there who haven't considered the huge benefits of such a trip. The upsides are terrific—a break from the family (who we love, of course, truly deeply), a chance to see a new city (and not during a business trip), and an opportunity to see the greatest sports team ever to exist in the history of Earth. It's one thing to go away and see the Mets or the Mariners, and fans of non-Yankee teams can use this book to good effect (the cities are the same, regardless of who's playing). But to go away and see the Yankees is something different. It helps that the Yankees generally win these games, so the trip pays off handsomely—Yankee fans can go, knowing in advance that by the end of the trip we can bask in victory and behave magnanimously toward the lesser among us, when they put up a brave fight but go down to inevitable defeat.

The trips are not so much fun when the Yankees lose—see the chapters on St. Louis and Chicago—but it's still a good time.

Let's get back to the cities for a minute—Yankee fans, especially those from New York, share the same arrogance about New York and its relationship to other American cities as we do about the Yankees and other teams. Our travels have confirmed that New York is the best city in the country. Nevertheless—and this is really important—the cities we've traveled to, and the people in them, tend to be really nice. The people are so nice, in fact, that it freaks us out. In Minneapolis, we actually started counting the number of people who said hello to us on the street and just started talking to us about baseball, New York, and anything else for no good reason. In St. Louis, a very nice lady walked halfway around Busch Stadium with us to show us our seats, I guess feeling that it was the neighborly thing to do. One of the best things about these trips is that the people we've met are friendly and interesting, they suffer Yankee fans with good humor, and they always seem quite happy to let us behave like jerks as long as we pay our way.

Cleveland's the exception, but you knew that. The people were fine, but Cleveland itself is a problem. More on that later.

So this book is about the away weekend. It's not that hard to do, especially if you tell your wife you love her before asking for time off. It's not that expensive, especially if one of the guys on the trip works for a major hotel chain (Steve has worked for Marriott forever, so he can get us affordable rooms at great hotels). And it's not all about baseball. I'm a political science professor with an interest in American history—baseball is a big part of these trips, but between games we have lots of time for museums, historical sites, and general checking-out of the cities and their character.

For me, this is a big part of why these trips work, and why they can work for diverse groups of people. We spend a lot of time talking and watching baseball, but we also spend a lot of time doing other things to keep the trips from getting boring or repetitive. There's more to do in any city than you can fit into a weekend, and so there's little time to get bored. And for the Clevelanders, if you're still reading, Cleveland has one of my favorite historical sites—the ridiculously oversized monument to assassinated nineteenth-century president James Garfield.

* * *

The book is arranged simply and directly. This first chapter offers some basics for picking an away series and getting started. Then the rest of the chapters cover our trips to various cities. We've thrown in a couple of cities we've been to without the Yankees. For

Yankee fans, though, these additional chapters will make a lot of sense—spring training in Tampa, nearby DC, and the minor league complex in Scranton. We threw Pittsburgh in, too, because that's where these trips started and because the city and its new ballpark are absolutely beautiful. Not so beautiful as our wives, of course, but worth seeing just the same.

The Basics

The outline of the trip is the place to start. This is much easier, we think, than people realize. Work schedules and family commitments shrink the number of weekends available for the trip. The baseball schedule itself offers limited options. Since I'm a professor and Steve has kids in school, we need to go in the summer—so no trips in April, May, or September. Since Steve has a regular job, he's limited to weekends. That leaves only away series on weekends in June, July, and August—and within those months, the Yankees are away only a handful of times, and only two or three series will find the Yankees in an interesting city. Many of the Yankees' summer weekends are taken up playing the Mets, playing divisional rivals in cities we see all the time (like Baltimore), or playing at home. We usually find only two or three away series that look promising, and then we can pick where to go and what will work with our schedules.

A basic rule: choose early, and *get tickets*. This locks the trip in, and protects it from later efforts to reschedule. The wife's sudden desire to take the kids to the botanical gardens, work's request that you come in on Saturday, and the kids' soccer game can all be blown off if you've already bought tickets, paid for the flight and the hotel room, and committed to going away with other folks who are relying on you. If you wait until the summer, look for cheap last-minute flights, or figure you'll buy tickets at the gate or from scalpers, you'll never go. Plan this out and lock it in over the winter when the baseball schedule comes out.

Getting tickets for the Yankees' away series can be difficult. The Yankees, for obvious reasons, are a huge draw on the road, and tickets can be few and far between. We hoped to go the Yankees-Dodgers series in LA one year, but couldn't get tickets we liked ahead of time without paying a small fortune. The Dodgers were very cagey about sales, and Steve and I both had trouble committing in advance to a West Coast trip. So it fell through. We got Kansas City as a fallback.

So for ticket availability, and to make sure the trip actually comes off, get tickets early and commit to the trip.

The away series are usually three games, and we tend to see all three. As a baseball fan, there is something very intriguing about watching an entire series live. It's a lot of baseball, but if you schedule it right it doesn't get boring. The third game can be a grind sometimes, but if it is you'll probably be looking forward to getting home to your family—not a bad outcome, really. (That's a good thing to tell your wife, too.) For a four-game, Thursday-to-Sunday series, we like going to Games 1 through 3, and leaving town Sunday. This gets us back to work on Monday, and ensures that we'll never have to watch Game 4 of a disastrous weekend sweep against the Bombers. (Again, see the chapter on Chicago.)

In general, and quickly, before we get on to the cities themselves, we tend to get there the day of Game 1, which is almost always a Thursday or Friday night game —check into the hotel, get squared away, and off to the game. We try to go early enough to wander around the stadium and check the place out, but with three games on the agenda there's no pressure to do that the first night. Game 2 offers sightseeing possibilities—if it's a night game, you have the entire day to see the city, then a nice relaxing night game. If it's a day game, there's usually time in the morning to do some sightseeing, then there's an opportunity postgame for a nice dinner and some time getting to know the city's nightlife. Game 3 is usually a Sunday day game—struggle out of the room, check out and stow your stuff in the car or with the concierge, see the game, and get on to the airport. Pretty simple.

Oh, bring back souvenirs for the kids. They like that.

Baltimore

Nicole has actually joined Steve and I at some of the games over the years. We all met when we all lived in northern Virginia in the late 1990s—the years of the Yankees' most recent dynasty. We used to make the 45-minute drive to Baltimore when the Yankees came to town. One time Steve and Nicole brought their newborn baby, Owen, wrapped up like a Christmas ham, so he could hear what 50,000 screaming Yankee fans sound like up close. But it was worth risking the deafness, I guess—we drove up to watch longtime Oriole Mike Mussina make his first start for the Yankees in Baltimore.

Which reminds me—let's not forget that these trips are about going to the games. Baltimore has always given us great games and a great environment, and with Buck Showalter in charge the O's are once again a force in the East.

Yankee games in Baltimore are a step removed from any other city we've been to. Baltimore gets flooded with Yankee fans making the drive down from New York. Yankee fans are loud and dominant at Camden Yards, and we always considered these games home games for the Yankees. I always find the noise and the atmosphere at Camden Yards awesome.

We started doing Baltimore back when the Orioles had some really successful teams. It's easy to forget now that the Jeffrey Maier home run that Jeter hit into the right field stands at Yankee Stadium, in the '96 playoffs—where it was caught, clearly in the stands and in all fairness by 12-year-old Jeffrey Maier, and there's no way that Tony Tarasco could have ever reached it even in his wildest dreams—that home run came in a tough playoff series against the Orioles. That shot began the Jeter legend and launched the Yankees' recently ended dynasty. The Orioles were really good back then, even with overrated Cal Ripken at short (we get up and go to work every day, too, my friend, and nobody's paying us millions of dollars). Camden Yards was always filled with noise and energy, like I've never seen anywhere aside from the old Yankee Stadium.

It's funny, I have almost no recollection of any game action from the games we saw in St. Louis and all the games we've been to in Pittsburgh—I remember great cities and great stadiums, but no recollection of the games themselves. Baltimore, for some reason, is different. Baltimore's always been about the baseball.

If you haven't been to Baltimore to see baseball, go. Camden Yards is generally given credit for being the first of the throw-back stadiums, brand-new but designed to look and feel like the intimate old parks of yesteryear. This design wave led to the new parks in Seattle, San Francisco, and other places, replacing the old cookie-cutter astroturf bowls with quirky, natural grass parks. The seats and the services in these parks are top notch. All of the seats at Camden Yards are terrific, and if you get hungry there's Boog's Barbeque and a range of food and beverage options that still outclasses most parks we've seen.

One year one of the Marriott hotels in Baltimore gave Steve tickets to their corporate seats at Camden Yards, which got us even closer than normal. We sat six rows back from the Yankees' dugout, and so very, VERY close to the players and the field. Not being rich guys, we don't get this kind of luxury very often, which is maybe why it stands out so sharply for both of us.

The image burned into both of our brains is the contrast between two great pitchers, Roger Clemens and Mariano Rivera. Clemens started—if you haven't seen him up close, you have no idea how big this guy is. He's huge. Not only that, but he's a human mountain of effort. He trudged back and forth to the mound as if carrying those 300 pounds of artificial bodymass took every muscle he had. And when he pitched, from up close you could see how he put every—last—ounce—of—effort into every pitch. He was grunting and sweating and using everything he had on every single pitch, like his life depended on it. He muscled his way through eight strong innings.

Then in comes Mariano Rivera, looking like a college kid walking across the quad. He's tiny by comparison—thin, even small-looking. Like a normal human being. But he comes in, tosses the ball toward the plate, and it jumps out of his hand like a dart. No effort, no straining, no grunting, just a little flip and a 95-mph cutter that you can barely even see. It's one of the most amazing things I've ever seen. Then he walks calmly off the mound, game over. It was a real treat to see this up close, especially having just watched Clemens expend ten times the effort to struggle, really work through the first eight innings. Then toss, toss, done, game over. Rivera's a freak.

At the same game we saw journeyman Glenallen Hill crack the most massive home run either of us have ever seen. To this day, I can hear the sound it made. Imagine the normal sounds made by bat and ball, but plugged directly into your brain and turned up to 11. I have three sounds permanently scored in my brain—a note I heard pianist Stephen Scott play once in Boston's Regattabar; the sound my skull made when I got hit in the face with a blistering one-hop grounder that took a bad hop (the ball rebounded off my eye socket at shortstop and went all the way into right field)—and the sound of the homer Glenallen Hill hit. It probably helped that we were only about 50 feet away when he hit it. And the thing traveled like you wouldn't believe. Monstrous shot. I can only imagine what that felt like to Hill when he hit it—probably like Reggie Jackson felt when he hit that moonshot in Detroit, or like Pujols felt when he crushed Brad Lidge in the playoffs.

Before this game started we were watching Chuck Knoblauch and Jeter taking their practice swings, as they were the first two batters up to start the game. Knoblauch was a head case who had major problems throwing the ball cleanly to first on routine plays. Playing second base, he used to field grounders and then throw the ball not to first, but often directly into the ground or ten rows deep into the stands. It was both funny and really, REALLY annoying. A similar tic had plagued Steve Sax, and Met fans will remember catcher Mackey Sasser's inability to toss the ball back to the pitcher. The problem drove Sasser out of baseball.

Anyway, at the time of the game Knoblauch was also having problems at the plate and was popping up A LOT, which was really pissing us off. We decided we should help. As he was warming up swinging his bat up and down vertically, almost as if he were digging a grave, we yelled "Hey POP-UP CHUCK! Swing the bat level...this is why you pop-up so much, you rube!" This went on for a few minutes with us laughing between yelling until we realized how pissed Jeter was at us. He gave us the cold death stare that Steve still remembers to this day.

* * *

Steve P. should have learned that talking to players doesn't usually bring good fortune. He's had a couple of run-ins with players. As he tells it:

Once in Boston, I was staying at the same hotel as the Yankees and saw John Wetteland signing autographs a few hours before the game at Fenway. As I waited on line to get an autograph, I saw Bernie Williams sitting in a cab yelling for Wetteland to hurry up. I thought about going over to Bernie to get his autograph instead, but figured Wetteland's would be worth more. This was back in 1994 and, in hindsight, definitely not true. I was the next in line to get an autograph when Wetteland announced that the one he was then signing would be his last. I said, "Come on John…one more." He then put his finger on my chest and said "I SAID, THAT WAS THE LAST ONE." I told him to RELAX, or something like that, perhaps something a little more aggressive, and he turned around like he wanted to kill me but thought better of it. I will always be a Yankee fan but have always wanted Wetteland to FAIL. Athletes need to draw a line, but don't be a jerk about it. It was nice to see him leave New York and finish a forgettable career. OMG…what will the Yankees do without John Wetteland? One word…Rivera!

I had an exchange in Baltimore, too. Once while hanging out over the Yankee bullpen at Camden Yards, David Cone tried to pick up a girl next to me. A bunch of us were talking to the players when Cone asked this hot girl standing next to me where she would be hanging out later. I jumped in and, pretending he was talking to me, told him "We're probably going to hit the hotel bar across the street." He jumped all over me and said "NOT YOU, HER" and pointed to the hottie. No shit, dumb ass, I was messing with you. They set up plans and she was pretty young. I know this because she was with her parents and she made sure it was OK to meet him later.

At the game where we saw Clemens and Rivera up close and watched Hill's home run, I also managed to get the stare-down from Tino Martinez. On his way back to the dugout after being in the field, Tino flipped a ball into the crowd where we were sitting. I always wanted to catch a ball and I just reached out and snatched it. Apparently Tino was flipping it to a kid nearby and when I picked it off I got another cold death stare, now from Tino. But that kid should have been faster.

* * *

Baltimore's a good city. Even though we've never done a full series weekend trip there, we're sure many people have. Baltimore's perfect for Yankee road trips. The city has a terrific aquarium, historic sites that include Fort McHenry (birthplace of the Star-Spangled Banner), and a successful Inner Harbor redevelopment of culinary and architectural interest. A neat little water taxi will take you around the harbor and over to the party area at Fell's Point, if you want to get away from middle-aged middle-America and their "children" at the Inner Harbor. And Baltimore, for whatever reason, really seems to offer a game experience that exceeds everywhere else we've been. It's a beautiful stadium, even now when it's been around for a while, and there's something about watching the Yankees on the road, in an away stadium dominated by Yankee fans, that we've never seen anywhere else.

St. Louis

Steve P. picks up the story:

I flew into Lambert St. Louis International Airport, and it had a convenient train from the airport to the Renaissance St. Louis Grand Hotel downtown on Washington Avenue. The train system was nothing fancy but served its purpose well. On the train from the airport, the conductor announced, "At the next stop, everyone must get off the train, it's going out of service." We all got off outside (not in the best neighborhood) for about 20 minutes until another train arrived to pick us up. Anywhere else, people would have been angry standing in the intense heat; some people were in business suits going to work. St. Louis people are super nice though, and I had a nice conversation with a guy going to work. He was telling me things to do while visiting and was seemingly unaffected by the delay. It definitely put me at ease.

I arrived a couple of hours earlier than Steve R. because of flight schedules. I had some work to finish up, which gives a different take on some of these trips than that presented by Steve R.—as a professor, he's usually pretty free from the office when we go on these trips. I usually have to fit the trip in around a regular job and the real world, which can be pretty different.

Before leaving for my baseball trip, my department at work was undergoing a restructuring and I was one of six people that had to interview for four positions…typical corporate nonsense. It was a stressful process and the hiring manager wanted me to be available on Thursday—when I'd be in St. Louis—for a follow-up call after my interview. He is definitely not the sports type and looked bewildered when I told him about why I was off from work on Thursday and Friday. I probably should have told him that I was visiting my grandmother or something but I didn't think quick enough, creating a little more stress for me. I got settled into this awesome hotel and called him. After some good conversation, he asked again why I was in St. Louis and there were some awkward pauses on the phone as I explained why we do this, so I quickly changed the subject to how nice the hotel was and how nice people were in the Midwest. Thankfully I got a job offer and accepted before Steve R. even arrived! This really set the table to have a relaxing and fun weekend!!

After closing up shop on work for the weekend, I asked where to find a bite to eat and they directed me to the St. Louis Bread Factory. You may have heard of Panera Bread…this is the original one and they created Panera off of this and shopped it around the country. This place is awesome for all meal periods. I ate there five times in three days which is a Panera Bread record (at least in my mind).

The Yankees lost 2 of 3 games to the Cardinals, but it was a great series and a lot of fun watching with the St. Louis fans. The fans actually would apologize for winning and spoiling some of our fun. This was far from the truth and it was crazy that they felt bad for us.

There was one drunk guy that got in my grill after Saturday night's win by the Yankees. We had fun watching Clemens get a win, and Albert Pujols had a rotten game. We kept asking everyone what the big deal was about him? He looks pretty feeble…they just laughed knowing that he was probably the best hitter in baseball at the time. Anyway, a guy after this game told me the Yankees suck and we asked him if he was feeling OK. We asked who was in the World Series from the National League the year before because it didn't even seem like they had a representative. This was the year after the Cards got swept by the Red Sox in 4 straight.

As he pointed out that the Yankees were to blame for blowing a 3-0 lead over Boston in the American League Championship Series, which caused the crazy momentum the Red Sox had, someone shouted "STEVE, it's DOUG." It was a guy that I knew from Long Island (where I grew up) that I had not seen in 10 years. He was doing the same thing we were, but with his entire family. They were staying at the Ritz Carlton, as were the Yankees, apparently. This was valuable information, because we were starting to realize that certain players needed to start hearing from us. Johnny Damon in Chicago, for example. This encounter basically stopped my conversation with this crazed Cardinal fan, which was great. To this day, any talk about the Yankees blowing the 3-0 lead to Boston in 2004 makes me sick to my stomach.

Right across from Busch Stadium was the Bowling Hall of Fame. Remember Earl Anthony and Mark Roth and Marshall Holman? It was actually cooler than you think. At the end you can bowl a full bowling game which we did before the Saturday afternoon game!

One thing we like to do is to see downtown and suburban neighborhoods to see how it would be to live in these cities. Steve R. had his car on this trip so one night we went out to Little Italy for dinner where we sold some extra tickets to the waitress at face value and then went further out to a bookstore. St Louis is a really nice city with friendly people and seemingly a nice place to live.

We saw the Arch, of course, but did the movie and not the elevator tour to the top. I am NOT a big fan of being trapped. The Arch has ancient elevators packed beyond capacity, crawling up to the top. I might have done it but was out of clean underwear.

* * *

It's funny, I don't have many impressions from the St. Louis trip in my head. Steve captures a lot of what I do have—I remember we ate almost every single meal at Panera, which was terrific. One night we headed out to Laclede's Landing, the big downtown hotspot area, to get a good dinner. I think we were both disappointed—it was a bit of a hike under the expressways to get there, and the place just seemed flat. Panera was much better.

It was also sweltering. Steve doesn't mention that not only would we have been trapped in the elevator death cars at the Arch, but we probably would have roasted to death before they got in to rescue us. The whole weekend seemed to be 100+ degrees, and every day before the games it seemed to threaten massive thunderstorms. Panera, however, was always nicely chilled.

I do remember making fun of Pujols. I remember screaming at him during the games, and calling him "Alice" pretty frequently. The fans were awesome—including the nice lady who walked with us halfway around old Busch Stadium to show us where our seats were, then she showed us where HER seats were. I guess in case we needed anything. Terrific people out there.

I don't have fond memories of the games themselves. The Yanks dropped two of three, as Steve says. Randy Johnson was awful, as he generally was with the Yankees, and the team just looked worn out. The Yanks were not having a great season—this was 2005—and they were struggling through the dog days. Seeing Busch Stadium was fun, though—a big part of our choice of destinations has been to see some of the stadiums before they're torn down. We managed to get to Minnesota before the Twins moved across town and the Homerdome collapsed, and we saw old Busch even as the new Busch Stadium was going up next door.

Two other notes on the margins are worth mentioning. Of course, we went on the Budweiser Brewery tour. This was fun, and the complex there is like a little city of beer. Plus, of course, free tastings.

The other thing is how we got rid of our extra tickets, which provides a good tip for these trips. We came to St. Louis with too many tickets—we'd overbought, with the idea that we'd scalp any extras and make some dough. It was Busch Stadium's final year, it was the Yankees, the Cards were great in those years—we figured we'd clean up.

Not to be.

Not only did we waste far too much time standing outside Busch in blasting, blazing heat trying to sell tickets to people who didn't want them, but the need to get rid of the tickets just weighed us down. From the minute we got to town, some of our planning necessarily had to account for the time it would take us to sell the extras. We had to figure where and when, and how much; we had to approach strangers; we had to worry about getting cheated, or arrested, or just shamed for panhandling. This is why we eventually gave the tickets to the waitress in Little Italy.

The Little Italy area is a wonderful neighborhood of great Italian restaurants overlooking the city—it's where Yogi Berra grew up! We'd been shut out of many of the restaurants in the main section of the neighborhood, which were all full up with long lines a-waiting. Once we got two blocks off the main drag, though, we found a wonderful little Italian restaurant with awesome food and a comely young server. We offered her the extra tickets we had for the next day's game. She declined, but she came back later and suggested that some guys in the kitchen would like them. My recollection is that we just gave them away. I know that we both felt great having got rid of the tickets, and the feeling of giving them away rather than letting them rot in our pockets for lack of a buyer was worth the monetary loss. Steve's right that I don't necessarily operate in the real world—I have no recollection of how much the tickets cost or what we lost on them, but I do hope that the guys from the kitchen got to the game and had a great time.

I hope that we'll get back to St. Louis to see the new stadium some day. And Steve's right to mention the number of people who make these trips. They're everywhere, and they have lots to say online about hotels, restaurants, where the Yankees stay, and so on. We certainly don't know everything about these trips, nor do we think we've stumbled on some kind of secret. But if you haven't done these trips yet, they're EASY: get the tickets—not too many—get rid of work to the extent possible, and enjoy the pleasant company of people in polite, well-adjusted midwestern cities. Eat at Panera, check out the neighborhoods, and don't expect guys like Albert Pujols to have too many bad games. I'm sorry I called you Alice.

Cleveland

Poor Cleveland. Even with a Championship, it's still Cleveland.

We actually had a good time in Cleveland, partially because the Yankees swept—allowing us to act like jerks all weekend, wearing our Yankee gear and high-fiving all the other Yankee fans in the streets and bars all night long after the games. But Jacobs Field—Progressive Field, as I write this; who knows what it is now—anyway, the Jake is an excellent place to see a ball game. The city, despite being heavily deconstructed while we were there, has lots of fun things to do, like the Rock & Roll Hall of Fame and the tomb of James Garfield. Cleveland really runs the gamut. And yet, somehow, Cleveland still struggles. Poor Cleveland.

We had wanted to see games in Cleveland for a long time. Back in the '90s, the Cleveland baseball team—I won't repeat their Jim Crow-era nickname here—they were actually good. Manny Ramirez, Carlos Baerga, Kenny Lofton, Omar Vizquel, Charles Nagy, Albert Belle—remember those guys? Great team, got lots of press for signing young stars to long term deals as a way of securing competitiveness in a small market. (Cleveland, by the way, is not a small market. You've got all of northern Ohio, and western New York if you wanted it. Stop whining.)

The other fun thing about Cleveland was—aside from one off year when Sandy Alomar Jr. touched up Mariano for a big home run—the Yanks owned Cleveland. Knocked them around every year. And it's centrally located, meaning you can probably do this trip in the car if you have the time. When Steve and I went, he was in northern Virginia and I was living in Flint, Michigan. We both drove, about 5 or 6 hours each, and met in Cleveland for the weekend series. It's about the same distance from New York, and 5-6 hours is do-able in one day even for middle-aged married guys. Driving home was even better. We both left right after the Sunday game, which the Yankees won, sweeping the weekend series. Unplanned, Steve and I both wound up driving out of town listening to Cleveland sports radio—for hours. It was hilarious the way they ripped their own team. They were SO mad.

But the baseball team deserved the criticism, I thought, as I headed back to the good life in Flint. Not only had the team dropped all three to the Yanks, but it wasn't close. Cleveland played badly, highlighted forever in my mind by Jhonny Peralta getting picked off first base by Andy Pettitte—with Cleveland losing, late in the game, Sunday—and with the bases loaded! I know Pettitte's good, but who gets picked off first with the bases loaded? Somebody on Cleveland, that's who. Poor Cleveland.

Maybe they should change the team's name.

This isn't a bad time for a digression on the name. Most people don't focus on this, and I won't spend a lot of time on my soap box. But Indian affairs is my research field, as a political scientist, and I actually teach the controversy over Native American-themed sports mascots in some of my classes. Many sports fans couldn't care less. Lots of American Indians care a lot.

The reason they care is not what we're usually told. The naming of sports teams and the use of mascot imagery based on American Indians or their leaders is not really an issue because it's "offensive", as if people's feelings are hurt and so giant corporations should be nicer. That's what's always reported, but that's not it at all. Many of the activists working to retire native-oriented nicknames point, instead, to actual social effects of perpetuating stereotypes—such as how Indians are depicted almost exclusively as young, warlike men—rarely women, rarely children, rarely seniors. Many of them point to the corporate mistruths put out by the team as it misrepresents the origins of the name. Many activists focus on the way such team names create hostile environments. This last one is really the key. Activists argue that using names like "Indians" and "Chiefs", especially in schools, creates a hostile learning environment for kids. Hostile learning environments are not only bad ideas, they're illegal.

These hostile environments, together with the stereotypes, discourage non-Indians from recognizing that the native population in America is in serious trouble. Suicide rates, dropout rates, poverty rates—all are off the charts in native communities. You'll notice that I use the term "Indian" as I write. Keep in mind, the issue is not that the word itself is offensive. Most American Indians I've met use that term and prefer it over the more PC "Native American"; established groups like the American Indian Movement, the National Congress of American Indians, and the Oneida Indian Nation use it, too. Using the word to identify the people is fine, in most cases. Using native words to identify places, like Massapequa or Chicago or Alabama, is generally fine, too. The use of it as a sports team's nickname, or to identify a mascot, in a way that encourages the stereotypes and gets people tomahawk-chopping and screaming that people need to be scalped—that's different. And unnecessary, really.

Lots of sports franchises and colleges and local schools have changed their names, with little effect on the bottom line or on fan support. Ask the Washington Wizards, who used to be the Bullets. Ask the University of Illinois, which retired their "Chief" a few years ago. Ask Syracuse or Stanford if retiring their Indian names and mascots destroyed their schools. The answer is, it didn't.

See, this is poor Cleveland's problem. Most of you are probably thinking, Enough of this crappy lecture—what happened to baseball roadtrips? But to get back to the roadtrip, you've got to go back to reading about Cleveland. Do you think that's going to be better? Only Cleveland could lose a battle for a reader's interest to a lecture on sports mascots.

Cleveland is a good city for this kind of trip. It's compact, and it has lots of things to do. The bar scene outside the stadium is terrific, and sits in a neighborhood right next to both the Jake and the Cavaliers' arena, making for maximum partying. Yankee fans were everywhere—we'd walk down the street after the games, and people would just start screaming *Let's Go Yank-ees!* and high-fiving everyone. It was a total takeover of the city. The hotel was packed with Yankee fans, the restaurants were packed with Yankee fans, even the Rock & Roll Hall of Fame was packed with Yankee fans.

The Hall is worth a look. It's smaller than we expected, but they have Billy Joel's scratched-up motorcycle on display just as you walk in, so they're alright. The Hall of Fame and Museum is disorganized, much like rock and roll tends to be, with a bizarre array of exhibits on everyone from The Who to Madonna to Peggy Lee. The displays are all over the place, too—clothing, guitars, television-art installations running old MTV videos. They have a terrific film that compiles clips of the Hall's inductees, and a wide-ranging gift shop. Most baseball fans don't need our advice to make a stop here, but if you're on the fence, go. It's at least worth a look. Just go early, because all those New Yorkers make for long lines.

The Rock & Roll Hall of Fame and Museum is also just a short walk from downtown—it's really *in* downtown, just by the water. It was about a 15 minute walk from our hotel, in the middle of the city, to the Hall. In the same complex are the Aquarium and the Science Museum, and also the Cleveland football stadium. I can't use the football team's nickname, either. (Paul Brown has seen the team play, and he's offended.)

This is not a bad walk around town. To our disappointment, though, the city itself seemed to shut down over the weekend. Most of the restaurants and stores were closed during the day, so there wasn't much to be done other than these sights. I've traveled a lot, but as a native New Yorker I'm still surprised that most cities aren't open all the time. Most downtowns shut down on the weekends.

Our other sight-seeing day in Cleveland took us out of downtown. We took their train system from downtown out to the 'burbs, to Case Western's campus area. Public trains are a great, cheap way to see a city. For a couple bucks max, we got a 40-minute aboveground, air-conditioned tour first of downtown, then of the surrounding area.

We were headed for the tomb of former president James Garfield. Steve indulged me with this one—it wound up being a much longer haul than I expected, for an obscure historical site. I loved it; I don't think he did. I learned to be more careful about my historical site destinations (the Negro Leagues Museum in Kansas City was a much better choice).

Anyway: Garfield is obscure, and probably most famous for being assassinated a short time into his term. Most people don't even know that, and if they do, don't care. So, after the train ride and another 45 minutes walking in summer heat through non-descript suburbs and a huge cemetery, we were shocked to see a gigantic tomb. It looked like a miniature US Capitol building—five stories high, huge dome on top, on top of a big hill, giant stone staircases leading up to it, the whole deal. It outranks every presidential tomb I've seen, with the exception of Grant's Tomb in New York.

It was hilarious. How in heck does *Garfield* get a monument like THIS??

We asked. Turns out—and this is one reason I love this monument—it turns out the people of Ohio loved James Garfield. He was a longtime, dedicated public servant. He literally gave his life to his country. We forget the commitments made by effective, public-spirited civilians these days. Garfield earned the love and respect of a huge community of people in Ohio, and they raised huge truckloads of money after his assassination in order to honor his service with a respectful giant monument. So Cleveland may kind of suck overall, but they kind of won me over with this one. LeBron will never get a monument like that, even if the Cavs win five more championships.

This cemetery, by the way, is really interesting if you like that sort of thing. F. W. Woolworth is buried there; so is Armour, of Armour hot dogs; George and Ira Gershwin; even Tony Randall.

The first game we watched in Cleveland involved rookies Phil Hughes and Joba Chamberlain. (That tells you how long we've been doing these trips.) This was one of the best things I've seen at a ballgame, and it really added to a weekend of baseball, rock-n-roll, and public service history. Hughes started Friday night, and went seven strong. He looked virtually unhittable, and showed the promise that would lead to his fixed place in the rotation a few years later. Joba came in late, and, without the stupid midges, mowed Cleveland hitters down. Jason Giambi pinch-hit a rocket of a home run over our heads into right field, and everybody was happy. Well, the 20% of fans who supported Cleveland weren't, but they didn't say much.

The seats at the Jake are great. We were initially down the right field line, in foul territory across from the right fielder, but Cleveland is one of those places where the seats are angled toward home plate. This means you don't have to twist your neck for three hours to see the game. Check it out next time they're on TV, right near the foul pole—everybody's angled toward home. This is a brilliant innovation; I'm surprised now when I see new stadiums go up that still have their seats pointed at the right fielder. Makes no sense. Score one for Cleveland!

But that's all they'll get. Saturday the Yankees won again, crushing the ******, 8-2. Sunday, Jhonny Peralta got picked off as they tried to launch a last-ditch effort to salvage something from a lost weekend. Too bad—I guess these guys lose most of their weekends in Cleveland, despite some recent success. Such a shame.

All things considered, Cleveland is a great place for one of these trips. It's close, it's got things to do aside from the games, it has ways to get to those things, it has good bars and restaurants and hotels, and it has tons of Yankee fans. What else do you need for one of these trips, anyway?

Minnesota

Minnesota was one of our best trips, and we look forward to going back to see the new outdoor stadium. Target Field opened in 2010, replacing the Homerdome—er, the Hubert H. Humphrey Metrodome—which is probably the wackiest baseball-watching experience we've seen. Together with the nicest people on Earth, Minneapolis is a terrific destination for watching the Yankees win games on the road.

Steve P. and I had wanted to see the Metrodome since we started talking about seeing road games. It always looked so weird on TV—a little dark, always the same, springy artificial turf, giant plastic baggie in right field. Crazy stuff.

The schedule, for some reason, rarely gets the Yanks to Minnesota in the summertime. Since Baseball went to the unbalanced schedule—meaning the Yanks often play the Twins just one series in New York, and one in Minnesota—for whatever reason the Yankees-Twins games always came off early in the year. April, for whatever reason, seemed the mandatory time for these games, maybe to capitalize on the interest left over from the Yankees' annual demolition of the Twins in the first round of the playoffs, which for a while seemed to happen every year. Whatever the reason, we feared that we'd never see a game in the dome, especially once the good people of the North set their caps for a new, outdoor stadium.

But then, there it was, in 2008—midsummer against the Twins. As we wrote in the introduction, the baseball schedule only offers a few weekends away in interesting places, and personal schedules pose obstacles, too. This one worked, though—Steve was able to do it, and I had planned to go to the National Conference for Media Reform, which that year was in Minneapolis—the weekend after the Yankees were in town. It was perfect—I could see the Yankees, then do some field research on Indian affairs in Minnesota, then come back to the city the following weekend for the conference. And we'd see the dome just before we ran out of time.

The itinerary was pretty standard by this time. Steve got us a room in a Marriott in the heart of downtown, and we flew in on Friday with tickets to Friday, Saturday, and Sunday. Steve would fly home Monday, and my idiot brother Dave would fly in—he was going to join me for a roadtrip through Minnesota, where he'd lived in the '80s.

Useful information: Minneapolis' mass transit is awesome. They have a little light rail train above ground which runs from the airport right into downtown, with stops at both the Metrodome and the Mall of America. When we got to downtown, it was only about a three block walk to our hotel. We used the light rail all weekend.

The people started to freak us out almost immediately. We decided to walk to the Friday night game, across the middle of the city. From the minute we got on the street, friendly people started engaging us in conversation! If you're from New York, this is an almost unheard-of breach into personal space. In New York City, asking someone if they're headed to a ballgame or if they're from out of town is usually translated as, "Please stab me." New Yorkers keep to themselves on the street (unless someone needs directions—we're not animals). When the Minnesotans started talking to us, we were bewildered.

The questions were basic and friendly. There's no reason we should have been upset by this, as we eventually realized. "You guys going to the game?" "Are you in from New York?" "Do you need directions to the Dome?" "Can I offer you a sandwich?" "Your shoe's untied—here, let me fix that for you." Seriously, almost everybody we passed talked to us. Now, surely we looked like we were from out of town, what with our Yankee hats, tourist map, and the don't-mess-with-me scowls we use in cities. But these people got right through all that. They were friendly and fearless. They didn't seem to think we'd stab them at all.

We actually started counting how many people talked to us in the mile-and-a-half walk from the hotel to the Dome. We lost count. This continued all weekend—on the street, at the games, in bars, even at the breakfast buffet.

First, though, the Dome itself. I feel sorry for people who never got to see a game here—unfortunately, you can't even see the Vikings there anymore. This was the craziest ballpark I've ever seen, and maybe one of the craziest buildings. It looks pretty normal on the outside, rather like a basketball arena. But what we didn't realize is that the soft roof of the Dome is held up by air pressure, a lot like a balloon. Giant electric fans blow throughout the game on the inside, to keep the roof up, at the same time creating a monotonous ambient roar beneath the crowd noise. When we sat up high, close to the roof behind home plate, we could hardly talk to each other.

These fans create a tremendous amount of air pressure, constantly blowing the roof upwards to keep it from flopping down. This means that the doors to the Dome, when closed, create a sealed bubble with air being forced to stay in and keep the roof up. Open a door—as in, when you're leaving after the game and need to get out—and the air literally pushes you out the doorway. The force is amazing—it's enough to knock down a small child or an old person. If you're a small old person, you're doomed.

The doors even have warning signs about how the pressure will affect you as you exit. Bizarre. But also one of the most fun things about the Dome.

The games in the Dome are weird, too. It's very much like being in a casino in Vegas—no clocks, no windows, no sense of time passing, no sense of a world outside. You're totally sealed in. Over the weekend we saw night games and day games, we saw games when it was clear and sunny and we saw a game while a wild storm raged outside. Aside from the slightest alteration in the light in the Dome, we knew nothing of any of this. It was like watching baseball in a womb, only we had to pay for our own food.

This was a lot of fun at first. When we first entered, I loved the place. It's neat and clean, the giant lower deck of seats offered great views of the field, and—maybe because of the dome—I felt very close to the field. It didn't hurt that we were, actually, very close to the field. The Twins' bullpen is down the third base line, one of those pens where the pitchers warm up in fair territory. The relievers sit in a covered area just in front of the stands. We were about ten rows back—close enough to yell at Joe Nathan when he got up to warm up. The Yankees were winning a close game, and Rivera had come in to close down the bottom of the ninth. Now, Yankee fans know that at this point the game is over. Nevertheless, and no doubt with some impossible hope of a Mariano meltdown, the Twins got Nathan up during the bottom of the ninth, just in case the Twins tied it and needed him to pitch the top of the tenth. We spent the next ten minutes yelling at Nathan to sit down—he wouldn't be needed. This was actually a lot of fun, because we were close enough that we hoped he could actually hear us. The good people of Minnesota thought we were awful boors. Too bad.

Nathan was not needed. The Yanks won the first game, 3-2.

* * *

Minneapolis is a great city. It's well organized, it has a terrific skyline, a historic riverfront, beautiful parks, and, of course, the light rail to get you around. We found that it's a great walking city, though—we took the rail when we needed to make time, but for the most part we walked the entire city in the couple of days we were there.

The city itself is built on the banks of the Mississippi River, which flows past downtown and separates Minneapolis from St. Paul—which we never got to. (Next time.) It's a historic city, and the waterfront includes a variety of museums dedicated to the city's industrial past—it was the center of the flour industry in the nineteenth century! Outside the city, as I found out the following week, are iron ranges, beautiful lakes, and lots of history from the Indian wars of the nineteenth century. Fort Snelling, on the river just south of the city, was an important fort during the United States' advance westward. The little city of Mankato, also south of Minneapolis, is the sight of the largest public hanging in American history. 38 Sioux Indians were hanged, following a brief war in western Minnesota and a series of kangaroo trials that led President Lincoln to commute the sentences of more than 300 people who had also been scheduled to hang.

We walked the city from downtown to the waterfront, and across the Stone Arch bridge. This gives you a good look at the city and the river—it's an impressive bridge, over rushing rapids, waterfalls, and curious industrial islands. On the other side you can walk through some less cared-for areas and construction sites, and make your way back across the river down by the Metrodome. We were there not long after the tragic collapse of the I-35 bridge, and we were able to watch fascinating construction of the new bridge going up in its place. The new Target Field is closer to the heart of downtown, in the center of the entertainment and nightlife district, so this route won't work that well anymore. But you can always check out the waterfront and the bridges, and then take the light rail back.

In the shadow of the Metrodome was a small cluster of bars, where we stopped for a beer and were forced into friendly conversation with staff and patrons. Lots of misguided Twins fans here, but still no stabbings! Also down here—and I wonder how it's doing with the Twins' relocation—was a terrific memorabilia store fat with all things Twins. The store celebrated the great Twins—Harmon Killebrew, Jack Morris, Kirby Puckett, Kent Hrbek. Cards, posters, vintage hats and photos—great stuff, in the kind of place you figure has been there forever. I hope it's survived.

We did all that on Friday, then Saturday took the light rail to the Mall of America. As in Cleveland, the above ground train was a great, cheap way to sightsee. The trains in Chicago and St. Louis were also terrific ways to get a sense of the place. The rail in Minneapolis took us right into the Mall of America, which we felt we couldn't overlook. Guess what? It's a shopping mall! Well, really, it's like four shopping malls one on top of another, but if you've seen a shopping mall already—well…

If you get down there, though, there are a couple of things not to miss. Skip the stores, unless you need gifts for the wife and kids. But don't miss the rides in the center of the mall. When we were there they had a surprisingly good, disorientingly fast blast coaster, and also a slower rollercoaster that affords excellent views of the Mall as you ride it.

In the middle of the ride area, we stumbled on a surprising find—home plate from County Stadium, where the Twins played before the Metrodome opened! We had no idea this was here, but of course that's part of the reason to take these trips and not just go to the games. The plate was set into the floor near the rollercoasters, with an explanation plaque nearby. A welcome surprise in the middle of a shopping mall.

* * *

Back to baseball. Saturday night the Yanks won again. Sunday they lost. Some of you may remember the signature moment from this game: Melky Cabrera falling on his rear end in centerfield chasing down a ball rolling into the right-centerfield gap. As he fell, he followed through with his throw back to the infield—resulting in one of the lamest throws you'll ever see from a major leaguer. The ball dribbled into short right-center field as Justin Morneau chugged around the bases for a triple and home on the error. Embarrassing.

Also in this game, we saw Twins pitcher Nick Blackburn get clocked in the head with a line drive off the bat of Bobby Abreu. Blackburn would be OK, but this was a scary moment. We watched it from our seats in the left-field bleachers, where when you watched on TV was where all the Yankees' homers used to go. Blackburn was on the ground for a long time, as we watched replay after replay on the TVs in the luxury seats.

The Yankees had won Saturday night. After that game, we found our way to the bar area near the hotel. For a while, we wandered the main nightlife area, where Target Field and Staples Center are now. This is dominated by expensive looking clubs, with lines, bouncers, and limos. No good for us—we just wanted a good bar to hang out in. We did find, for a while, a *Sex and the City* party. This just added to the feeling of oddness all weekend, what with the Dome and the friendly people and all the flour factories. We'd noticed an alarming number of young women wearing weird, prom-style party dresses on the streets, and didn't know if this is just what people did on a Saturday night in Minneapolis. We finally figured out that the *Sex and the City* movie had premiered that weekend, and a bar downtown was having a big release party. We crashed that for a while, but—like the movie, we assumed—it was profoundly lame. Adding to the oddity of it all, though, was the focus of these Minnesotans on a Hollywood depiction of New York City, which we knew to have little in common with real New York. So there we were, New Yorkers in Minneapolis, dealing with all the friendliness, and the Minnesotans were pretending they were in New York. Weird.

We finally settled in at a different set of bars, up Lasalle Avenue near South 10th and 11th Streets. This is a great area—the bars have adults in them, with good food and great ambiance. Remember, this is a book for married guys, not for college trips. If you're 22 and looking to score, go back to the limos and the lines and the strip clubs. Steve and I were more comfortable with the adults in the Irish bars on the southwestern edge of downtown.

It's important here to note that Steve and I don't generally choose to talk to strangers. Steve has a sales background, so he's comfortable with meeting people, and sometimes even seems to enjoy it. I'm a hermit by nature—I want people to leave me alone.

This is why Minneapolis freaked me out so much. In one bar, we basically got involved in baseball discussions with lots of folks, proving that even if you don't want to get sucked into the locale, you will. And it was one of the best outings we've had on these trips.

One guy saw Steve's Yankee hat, stumbled over, and blurrily tried to look Steve square in the face. After a pause, the guy just said: "You guys will NOT make the playoffs this year." (Turns out, he was right.)

We also had a long conversation with a young couple, probably in their twenties, about baseball and Minneapolis. They were great fans—they understood the game, pleasantly defended the Twins, and praised the constant wisdom the Twins show in the moves they make (this was the season after the Twins traded Johann Santana to the Mets for Carlos Gomez, Philip Humber, Kevin Mulvey, and Deolis Guerra. Make up your own mind). The couple even showed great respect for the Yankees, much to their credit. We wound up giving them two extra tickets we had. Sometimes, through StubHub and other mechanisms, we've wound up with an extra pair of tickets. Steve and I had been wondering what to do with our extra tickets in Minneapolis, until we met these nice people. We'd had such success in St. Louis just giving the extra tickets away, that we did it again. These folks had mentioned that they might try to get to Sunday's game, and they really seemed like nice people. So we gave them our extra tickets. Good people in Minnesota—karma's a good thing.

The last guy I remember also just started talking to us because he knew we were from out of town. He turned out to be a maitre-d' at a steakhouse in the city, and he said the Yankees always came in for dinner. He actually seemed believable, and he invited us to come to the steakhouse for dinner the next night. He promised he'd introduce us to Joe Girardi and the coaching staff. We almost did this, and we talked about it all the next day. I think now I'd vote to do it, but at the time neither of us really wanted to bother Girardi, assuming the guy's story was true. Sure, it might be fun for us—but does Joe Girardi really want to have to deal with us when he's having dinner? Doubtful.

I say we'd probably do it now because I think Steve and I are slowly inching toward becoming stalkers. One goal for the Kansas City trip in 2010 was to find out where the Yankees stayed—a year after we tried to track down Johnny Damon in Chicago in 2009. He'd had a terrible game and we wanted to tell him how much he sucked.

The Yankees as a team sucked in Chicago. That was the worst trip we've done, because even with all the sightseeing, the point is still the games. The trips are great when the Yankees win, as in Cleveland and Minneapolis. The trips suck when they lose. In Chicago, they lost. And lost. And lost.

Chicago

    Chicago was one of our worst trips, and we don't look forward to going back.
    For some reason, I had a feeling Chicago might not work out. First, we'd had such good luck on previous trips—weather, logistics, the games, everything had always gone just right. We were due for an off year. Second, I'd been to Chicago numerous times. I lived in Michigan for five years and Chicago was close and always a good city, so this trip, for me, lacked a lot of the newness and anticipation that has accompanied our trips to more exotic locales like Minneapolis and St. Louis. Finally, Steve's family was considering getting a dog. Not a good time for him to be out of town. The Chicago trip went from a murmur of foreboding, to a dismal performance by the Yankees, to a vain search for Johnny Damon in the middle of the night.

    Chicago is a terrific city. What's more, it's a terrific sports city. The trip got off to a great start when Steve's contacts at Marriott in Chicago invited us to go to a Cubs game with them. Now, as I've said before, Marriott has treated us really well on these trips. They have a great record on the Americans with Disabilities Act, too—

one of my students did a senior thesis on the ADA, and found that Marriott has a real commitment to the ADA's goals, and in the academic literature Marriott is a case study for how that legislation can work to help both companies and people.

So we were not surprised that our new friends from Marriott were as nice as they were, or that Marriott's seats at Wrigley Field were as good as they were. First class all the way. We were in the third row from the field, directly behind home plate. Great seats. Our Marriott friends said that their left-out colleagues back at the office watched the game and saw us on TV the whole time.

As a quick aside, if you get to Chicago to see the Yankees play the White Sox, try to make a trip up to the North side to see the Cubs. This is no great insight to baseball fans, of course, but Wrigley meets expectations. Even if you can't get in to a game, the neighborhood up there is awesome. It's on a human scale, with the stadium set in an urban neighborhood stuffed full with bars, beer and wing deals, outdoor patios, and thousands of pretty young people playing hookey from work and having a good time. And not in a dangerous, drunken kind of way—just in a happy, backyard-buzz-in-the-summertime kind of way.

Cubs tickets used to be surprisingly easy to get. This may have changed, as the neighborhood has seen some changes in recent years, and as the Cubs' 2016 World Series Championship may have made it a lot tougher to just walk up and score tickets. But a few years ago when I was in Chicago with some friends, we decided to go see Wrigleyville (we hadn't been there before this). The Cubs were playing an interleague day game—against the White Sox, so we had little hope of buying tickets. We figured we might go up to about $50 if we could find a scalper, by which I mean a licensed, authorized reseller. We got off the lovely little above-ground train—after a great tour of the city out the window—and immediately we saw dozens of licensed, authorized resellers hawking tickets. This was about 15 minutes before game time, and we got good seats in the lower deck for face value, plus about a $5 gratuity to the brokers for their trouble (not for the tickets themselves, of course). This meant, ultimately, that we got in for about $30 a ticket—a great value, if you consider that we got to see a good, crosstown rivals game in the oldest stadium in baseball. The point is, take a run up there if you have time—you might get lucky.

On our trip, we had Yankees-White Sox tickets for Thursday-Friday-Saturday. The Cubs game was Thursday afternoon, so right after flying into town and taking the train directly from Midway Airport into downtown and checking in at the hotel, we headed out for Wrigley. Like Minnesota, the fact that the train goes directly into downtown from the airport makes this kind of a trip to Chicago really easy. Since Wrigley, and new Comiskey Park, are quite a ways from downtown Chicago where our hotel was, we got pretty familiar with the El.

Wrigley is a great baseball environment inside the stadium, too. People sing, they cheer, they pay attention to the game. There's no Ferris wheel, no Boog's Barbeque, no centerfield martini bar. Just the game, which was fun. The Cubs spanked the Astros, meaning that, by the time we left town on Sunday, Chicago was 4-0 in games we saw. Later that summer, we'd see the White Sox beat the Yankees in our first trip to the new Yankee Stadium. The next year, we saw the White Sox beat the Nationals in my first trip to Nationals Park, when we saw Stephen Strasburg's second start. We are, obviously, good luck for the White Sox.

After the Cubs game, we got a quick dinner outside Wrigley and got back on the train, all the way through the city and down to the

South Side, where some genius put the new Comiskey Park. I don't know what Comiskey does for the locals down there, but it's a pain in the ass to get there and back to a game. New York fans can associate this with Shea, and now Citifield. It's nice to get out of the city a bit, I guess, and the Mets have always been a team for the Long Island suburbs. Maybe the Sox serve the same purpose for Chicago's South Side, but to be honest, it makes it tough for outsiders to get there. Maybe that's part of the point.

The subway trip south is not exactly scenic, right along the expressway, and it takes about a half hour from the heart of Chicago. That doesn't include the twenty minutes we spent waiting for a train to get there, and the 45 minutes we spent trying to funnel into the subway stop outside the ballpark on the way home. This was ridiculous, actually, and added to our sense all weekend that this was not our best trip.

New Comiskey—sorry, US Cellular Field—sorry, Guaranteed Rate Field—is pretty non-descript. Physically, it's like many of the stadiums built in the last 20 years. It looks nice. But the general features are uninteresting. Despite the pinwheels, left over from old Comiskey, the place is functional and ordinary. A mostly symmetrical field, some prints of famous Sox players on the outfield wall, the flat-fronted pressbox behind home, a restaurant in an outfield corner. If you changed the color scheme and allowed yourself to be distracted, you could easily imagine yourself in Nationals Park, Comerica, or—gasp—new Yankee Stadium. Seriously, if you've been to both, the next time you're in Yankee Stadium imagine that all the white facings of the decks and the storefronts are painted black. US Cellular, right? It's too bad, really, that the parks have become cookie-cutter again, just like in the Three Rivers-Riverfront-Shea-Veterans Stadium days of uniform circular stadiumbowls.

OK. With the Yankees ahead of the Red Sox by 3 ½ games coming in, these games were July 31, August 1, and August 2. So the summer is heating up, the Red Sox are closing, Sergio Mitre and Joba are struggling in the rotation, and the trade deadline looms Thursday night. There's hope that the Yankees will get some wins against Chicago, which had just finished a 1-6 road trip. There's hope that the Yankees will get some help with a trade for a starter or a slugger to help them in the second half. Jake Peavy's available; so is Cliff Lee.

Our seats Thursday night are in the left field bleachers. Not bad, really—good view of the field and the Stadium itself, and we're among crazy bleacher dwellers on the South Side. Andy Pettitte pitched great, but some sloppy defense by the Yankees had the Bombers trailing 2-1 in the ninth. It was a frustrating game to watch—Pettitte was great, but the Yanks just couldn't get anything done. One of those nights where you don't expect much, but the pitching keeps you close. It's tough to watch a game lost because of bad fielding. So everybody was packing to go home as Nick Swisher stepped up with two outs in the ninth. He was awful all night, and we had been talking all night with the Sox fans about how he couldn't hit to save his life. They love him in Chicago, where he used to play, but they'd traded him for a reason. We weren't sure yet about him—he was still new to us, and his most famous Yankee moment so far had been striking out Gabe Kapler in an early season blowout when Swish had been called upon to pitch. Jorge Posada had to yell at him after the game, to remind him that the Yankees are about winning, not gimmicky strikeouts in embarrassing losses.

So everybody's packing up with two outs and now two quick strikes on Swisher, when he shocks the stadium by cracking a line shot into the leftfield bleachers, the next section over from us. The air went out of the place, expect for the scattered Yankee fans who were going nuts. Tie game, 2-2. Maybe a frustrating night could be salvaged, after all.

Then Hughes and Phil Coke gave it right back. Game over, Sox win 3-2. 20 minute walk to the subway stop. 45 minute wait to get to the platform. 15 minute wait for a train. 30 minute ride back into town.

It didn't get better. We spent the rest of the night in the hotel bar watching news of last-minute trades made at the deadline. Hoping for Cliff Lee, or Peavy, or someone. The White Sox got Peavy. Phillies got Lee. Roy Halladay went nowhere. Matt Holliday went to St. Louis. Billy Wagner went to Boston.

The Yanks got Jerry Hairston, Jr.

And scheduled Sergio Mitre to pitch Friday night.

After seeing two games in two parks on Thursday, we got away from baseball for a while Friday. We did a walking tour of Chicago's waterfront, which is a terrific way to spend a nice summer day. Our hotel was up on the Miracle Mile, a few blocks west of Navy Pier. We walked down to Grant Park first. We'd signed up for a tour of Buckingham Fountain, a historic main fountain in the park. It's been decaying for years, and there's a foundation working to restore it. For a $50 contribution, we got a behind-the-scenes tour of how the thing works. They showed us the control room, and let us play with turning various taps on and off to make the water do entertaining things. Operators used to control the whole fountain manually during shows, before computers could be programmed to take those guys' jobs. We also saw the bowels underneath the fountain, which looked like the final scene in half the slasher movies I've ever seen—dripping pipes, bad lighting, and weird corners where people obviously lived. Spooky.

We walked down the waterfront to the Aquarium area, and got a good look at Soldier Field. It's always fun to see these things live—it makes watching games on TV a little more interesting. We took the water taxi back up to Navy Pier—a good expenditure of a few bucks. Chicago's a water-oriented city, and one that appreciates and rewards architecture. The skyline seen from Lake Michigan is extraordinary.

Navy Pier is fun—probably more fun with kids. It's basically a big shopping mall jutting into the water, with a few rides and lots of overpriced restaurants. Even so, this is where we first started talking about doing a book. Maybe we realized that the current trip was lame, and we figured we'd rather talk about the other trips. Maybe we figured we'd better write it down before all the trips started to suck.

If this all sounds pretty lame, I suppose it was. Two games Thursday may have been a bit much. The Yankees were going in the wrong direction. It was hot. Steve was on the phone every twenty minutes talking to his wife and daughter about the dog. Adopt the dog, don't adopt the dog, what kind of dog, get the dog, don't get the dog. And, having been to Chicago many times, as I said, I'd seen much of this before. I think these trips definitely reward covering new ground. I advise anyone doing this and going to a familiar city to see new stuff—don't take your friends to the stuff you've seen before.

But we had high hopes for Sergio Mitre! And our newest midseason pickup, the great Jerry Hairston, Jr.! Cashman had done it again! First Fielder, then Justice, and now—Hairston! JUNIOR! To the ballpark!

20 minutes waiting for the train. 30 minutes to US Cellular. 20 minutes into the stadium. The Yanks would face DJ Carrasco, an emergency starter after Clayton Richard was sent to the Padres in

the Peavy deal. Yanks got up 3-0 in the first inning. Hairston was in the lineup, and paying dividends already.

Three hours later, the Yanks had lost, 10-5. Hairston actually made a nice catch, and did some good things on the bases. Later in the year, he'd make some nice role-player contributions. We made our peace with him.

But Mitre was awful, and it was 5-3 Sox by the 3rd inning. Alfredo Aceves gave up four in the 7th. Jayson Nix stole home for the White Sox. A-Rod got thrown out at second in the 9th, trying to stretch a single into a double with the Yankees down by 5 runs.

20 minutes back to the subway. 45 minutes to get to the platform. 25 minutes waiting for a train. A PACKED train. 30 minutes back to downtown.

Chicago nightlife is not what we found in Cleveland, St. Louis, or Minneapolis. Since the Stadium is so far from the central nightlife in Chicago—and since it's such a big city with so much going on—Yankee fans were rare, and nobody really cares very much about baseball. We made the mistake of going out right from the game, which meant that we were still in Yankee gear, caps, sweating, and in bad shape for clubbing. We actually got kicked out of one place. *After* they'd let us buy $10 beers, of course.

The other place that stands out was a bar full of kids, probably mid-twenties at the oldest, slamming shots and screaming and dancing. Steve and I are kind of past this at this point. This is where we decided we need to do more research for these trips now, and find bars that are better suited to men of a certain age, as it were. We just can't hang out with these kids anymore. As suited this weekend in Chicago, we never did find a good place to hang. Rush and Division has some good clubs, and even some good bars for adults, but it just never seemed to work. As I said, we were due. We'd had such good luck in St. Louis, Minneapolis, even Cleveland, we couldn't get too upset about a slightly off trip to Chicago. My best guess is that Chicago is spread out, it's a real city, and people live here. Chicagoans undoubtedly know where to go. We didn't.

Saturday, after Steve talked to his wife and daughter about adopting a dog, we wandered back to town with the plan of taking a harbor tour or a river tour. We took an absolutely awesome architecture tour on the river, which floated us lazily through the heart of the city as a brilliant guide told us about the buildings and the city's history. It was hot, and it rained for a while, and through half of the lecture Steve talked to his wife and daughter about adopting a dog, but this is still a great thing to do. It's low impact, restful, outdoors, educational, and it has nothing to do with baseball.

Then: 25 minutes waiting for a train, 30 minutes to the Stadium, 20 minutes to get inside.

Awaiting us inside? AJ Burnett. And not the good AJ Burnett. The Sox got 6 runs off Burnett in the second inning. They put up another 6 in the 8th. They had 17 hits. The Yanks lost, 14-4.

This was awful. I remember turning to Steve as Burnett walked off the field in the fifth, and saying, "Look at him flexing his arm. Maybe he's hurt." Steve just said, "He better be."

AJ gave up 10 hits. He couldn't get anyone out. He walked Jayson Nix with the bases loaded. Twice.

The rest of the team was no better. Posada tagged a guy at home with his glove hand—while the ball was in his bare hand. Safe. On second with the bases loaded in the 6th, Posada let himself get deked by the left fielder on a short fly ball. He held up, the ball dropped, and Jorge got forced out at third. Shelley Duncan had been sent down to the minors, in favor of Girardi favorite Cody Ransom. Ransom struck out three times to end innings, and left five runners on base. Girardi left Damon, Hinske, and Matsui on the bench all day.

20 minutes back to the subway, 45 to get to the platform, 30 back into downtown…

We saved Saturday night with a trip to Billy Goat Tavern, famous as ground zero for the Cubs' curse. The owner and his goat were supposedly ejected from Wrigley in 1945. The owner cursed the Cubs, saying that the Cubs would never win a championship until the goat got into Wrigley. The Cubs, even though they've tried, have never been able to make this right. (Even the Cubs' World Series win doesn't convince me that the goat is satisfied yet.) The food at the Tavern is basic burgers, but it's a throwback atmosphere—inner city grill, under the surface of the Earth. Hard to find, but definitely worth the trip.

The best parts of this trip were on either end of it: a near riot in the bleachers Thursday, and the stalking of Johnny Damon Saturday night.

Thursday, in the bleachers, something had upset some of the fine people in the section. A long, protracted argument developed that eventually included people our age, what looked like their kids and parents, vendors, and security guards. Remarkably, security let the bouts of screaming and fist shaking go on for 15-20 minutes, as the tension level wavered between cooling off and exploding into a riot. We never did know what caused the fracas. But in New York, the slightest hint of a disagreement usually brings overwhelming security and law enforcement, and leads to the immediate removal of anybody in a fifty-foot radius. They don't clown around in New York, and the cops don't negotiate.

In Chicago, though, the arguments just went on and on, as the nearby crowd screamed, inexplicably, "THROW THE WHITE TRASH OUT! THROW THE WHITE TRASH OUT!" The incident still makes no sense to me.

At the tail end of the trip, Saturday night, we were frustrated, angry, and at a loss what to do. Steve's wife and daughter had adopted a dog while he was out of town. I'd learned almost nothing from this trip, even with the architecture tour (I forgot everything the minute I got off the boat). We never found a good bar, we'd had few interactions with interesting people, and the Yankees' losses were just getting worse and worse.

As we were getting into the hotel elevator, though, ready to call it a night, a woman told us she'd just seen Johnny Damon outside another Marriott. She said he seemed a bit inebriated. We said he sucked. We decided we should talk to him. And tell him how much he sucked.

So we walked to a different Marriott. Then another Marriott. We got a drink in the hotel bar, fully convinced—wrongly—that this was where the Yankees were staying. Damon needed to hear from us. We weren't drunk—just mad. We realized that, from now on, we needed to find out where the Yankees stay, in case they need our advice. If we're no longer suited to doing shots with college girls, we ARE suited to being middle-aged losers haunting sterile, overpriced hotel bars, waiting to tell CC Sabathia how to pitch or Joe Girardi how to manage his bench. We never did see Damon, though. Or anyone else. We did have a nice chat about Chicago with the waitress, for about an hour. We think she probably got fired afterwards, because we saw her getting yelled at by her boss.

I hope Ozzie Guillen and the White Sox enjoyed this weekend.

Of course, the Yankees opened the new Stadium that year, and won the World Series. It's a long season; we just picked the wrong weekend. Tough. When we settled on Kansas City the following year, we had high hopes. And this time, we knew where the Yanks were staying.

Kansas City

Kansas City is where we finally stalked the Yankees. As we kind of suspected, it was worth doing—once.

As with all of our trips to the Midwest, the people were terrific—helpful, calm, good sports, and friendly. Guys our age know Kansas City from watching games on TV, on which the Royals' stadium used to show up as beautifully as any place the Yankees went. Two visuals stand out in my memory. The first was the highway in the background, past the outfield, which just suggested open space and almost a small-town summertime every day attitude about baseball. Plus, I liked the idea that this big league stadium was right next to a medium-sized highway with almost no traffic. Ever. Paradise for a New Yorker.

The other memorable visuals were the fountains. Back in the day, the Royals' stadium had beautiful, cool, spouting fountains ringing the outfield. Someone hitting a home run into the water was a thrill here long before the pool in Arizona opened up. And it just looked like such a wonderful place to watch a game, against a team with a stellar reputation for doing the best it could with limited resources. (And they used to have George Brett, the second-best third baseman in the AL in those years.)

Before we arrived, we had no idea how diminished the fountains have become, thanks to a misguided effort to remodel the stadium. It's still nice, with a wrap-around open concourse modeled on newer stadiums allowing you to stroll around the entire stadium and never lose sight of the game. The food was excellent, especially the doughnuts in the left field bleachers.

But the fountains have been cut down, and now, rather than defining the stadium, they seem like just another "feature" trying too hard to add character to a cookie-cutter ballpark—like the warehouse in San Diego, or the deeply lame Monument Park in the new Yankee Stadium. And what we found out is that Kansas City is hot—*hot holy crap it's hot*—hot. Sitting at the games in the afternoon was like sitting a foot away from the sun—blinding and viciously uncomfortable. I can only imagine how the fountains, in an earlier age, would have taken some of the sting off of summer on the plains. Now, there's almost no relief. Steve and I actually negotiated who was going to sit closest to the sun, allowing the other a few brief spots of 105-degree shade.

The games themselves were fine, if not memorable. The first night, we had seats in the first row overlooking the Yankees' bullpen in left field. Unfortunately for us, Sabathia pitched great, and so we didn't see anyone even stir in the bullpen until deep into the eighth inning. The relievers did throw a lot of sunflower seeds at each other, though. After watching him warm up, we both figured we could hit off of Sergio Mitre without a problem.

More than the games, the fans in KC stand out. The first night, the couple sitting next to us—after finding out that we were actually from New York—asked us about the Islamic Cultural Center being built near Ground Zero in New York. This astounded me. The "ground zero mosque," as it was called in the "news," was at that time the hot-button issue manufactured for the 2010 midterm elections. I was astonished that here we were, halfway across the country at a ballgame with very few actual New Yorkers, as far as we could tell, and the first discussion we had with the locals was about an issue unfolding in lower Manhattan. Why did these people care? And why did they care *so much*? And why did they parrot FOX News so closely? But these folks were the ones who suggested the doughnuts, so they're OK with me.

The next day featured a three-and-a-half-hour rain delay, so we got lots of time to talk with the locals. My favorite was a gentleman and his son, who had driven down from Omaha to see the game. They had some loose ties to Joba Chamberlain, and, bless their hearts, they were going to wait out the rain delay as long as it took before driving the three and a half hours back to Nebraska. The Yankees, in fact, have strong ties to the region, and there are homegrown Yankee fans all over Kansas, Nebraska, and Oklahoma. Later on this trip I went to the Phillips Oil Museum in Bartlesville, OK, and had a long discussion with some retired workers who had grown up with Mickey Mantle. They regaled me with back-in-the-day stories, especially of Mantle's off-season exploits when Billy Martin and other buddies came to visit. Always talk to the locals.

OK, on to the stalking.

For years, Steve and I had joked about trying to track down various players on these trips, and we'd come close to trying in Chicago. In KC, we decided we'd actually do it. We honestly didn't expect much—it was as much just a goal to help occupy our time in KC as anything else. Steve had a vague idea about getting an autograph for his son, but neither one of us was committed to that, or to talking to the players, or really anything. I think, at bottom, neither of us really want to bother these people, which explains our unwillingness to intrude on Girardi's dinner at the steakhouse in Minneapolis.

Nevertheless, we wanted to see if we could find the Yankees. I was curious to see how fans behaved when tracking down the Yankees—so I was actually much less interested in stalking the Yankees, and much more fascinated by the prospect of stalking a bunch of fans stalking the Yankees.

When we caught up with the Yankees after Saturday night's game, long after the rain delay had made for a very late night, we did get a few surprises. We had located the Yankees' hotel that afternoon, when driving around sightseeing. After the game Saturday night, we zipped over to the hotel. The hotel had a somewhat private drive that swung by the front door, then circled back out to a side street. When we got there, we found a dozen or so well-mannered fans standing behind a classic red velvet rope. This struck me as a marvel of crowd control. The rope was set back about fifteen feet from the door—but on only one side of the doorway, and the rope itself was only about eight feet long. So if one wanted, one could easily walk to the other side of the front doors and wait for—and approach—any arriving players. Or just walk around the rope when anybody showed up. Amazingly, nobody did this. Aside from a few folks sitting on a bench on the non-roped side of the front door, everyone stood calmly behind the rope and caused no trouble. They made very little noise, just normal conversation. Most of the adults had kids, and most of the kids had balls they hoped to have signed. One guy had a book full of cards and signatures, to which he was clearly hoping to add. But there were no freaks, no drunks, no loudmouths, and nobody disrespecting the rope. The rope ruled.

The fans remained calm and respectful when a few players started to come by. There was no calling, no booing, no demands for autographs—just respectful light applause, a mild cheer here and there, and a calm determinism to stand behind the rope in hopes that a player might, unbidden, come over to chat or sign. None of the players did. We saw just a handful of players, including Robinson Cano, Ramiro Pena, and Sergio Mitre, the rest evidently accessing the hotel through other passages—and then it was all over.

One moment really stands out, though. Dustin Mosely was a young pitcher who'd been called up to fill in for some of the Yankees' injured starters. Prior to KC, he'd been pitching surprisingly well—workmanlike performances that won games. He'd had a few rougher starts just before the KC series, and it looked like maybe the league was catching up to him. He had started that day in KC—and he hadn't pitched well. Mosely arrived at the hotel with a woman we took to be his mother. They got out of their SUV in front of the hotel, and Mosely just looked tremendously sad and disappointed. All of a sudden I had some marginal recognition of what this all must mean to a young player on the edge of the major leagues. His mom gave him one of the sweetest hugs I've ever seen, and then he went into the hotel and his mom drove away. It was a nice moment. Not at all what you expect to get when you go stalking professional athletes. But it reinforced our basic position, governing us for many years, that we should just leave these people alone to do their jobs and lead their lives.

After KC, we decided it might be time to get back to a little east coast mayhem—Boston. But before we leave the oppressive heat of Kansas City in July, a few words about the city as a destination. KC turned out to be really very interesting. The highlight is the Negro Leagues Baseball Museum, which is easy to find downtown and interestingly combined with the KC Jazz Museum. The Negro Leagues Baseball Museum is a must-see—it's small, but direct, with a film and some great exhibits. I picked up Robert Peterson's book, *Only the Ball Was White*, which is a very, very good read on the Negro leagues. For baseball fans in KC, this is an essential stop.

Also fun was the small but quirky Airline Museum, near the downtown airport (not the big airport we flew into). Exhibits included a display on stewardesses' uniforms, rules for passengers on early flights (like don't throw your cigarettes out the window over wooded areas), and some cool old planes. What struck us most is how little has changed in passenger accommodations in fifty years—the old airline planes had fold-down trays, bins for overhead luggage, and coffee pots and small galleys—almost exactly like today. Two major differences stood out, though—they used real dishes, and they had space to sit in the seats. Today, airlines jam double the number of seats into the same space. And no dishes.

Fine.
KC good. Go if you get the chance.
Boston next.

Boston

Steve P. picks up the story:

To start out, I was really not looking forward to seeing the Yankees in Boston. We tried to avoid it by looking at the Seattle Mariners series in May, the Angels in June or even the Cincinnati Reds in a mid-week series in June. A mid-week series would have broken our long tradition of road trips on weekends, but I wanted to do anything to avoid the cesspool of Boston. I even called in a favor from a friend in Chicago, who knew someone in Cincinnati, who happened to know Dusty Baker. We would have had great seats and stayed in a hotel within walking distance of the "Great American Ballpark".

As it turned out, I got a new job position at work and really couldn't take time off so early into starting. I know Boston is a nice city filled with great sports fans, but the thought of being harassed all weekend by mindless Red Sox fans sounded really unappealing. It's probably the biggest rivalry in sports and the Yankees were not faring well against Boston that year. In the end, though, Boston was the only option, so off we went! I went into this with an open mind and was determined not to argue with anyone; I told myself that I'd only fight if someone hit me first or did something very unpleasant to me. My family was extremely nervous for my safety.

I was coming from Northern Virginia and decided to fly, while Steve R. drove up from New York. While at Dulles Airport outside DC, I saw a couple that were Yankee fans that were waiting for the same flight to Boston. The woman had a Yankees jersey on, with the #1 and the name F-BOSTON on the back. I asked her if she was going to the game that night and she replied "I wish" and I followed up with, "Would you wear that shirt?" She looked me right in the eye and said, "I always do, because we love beating the shit out of people." There was no joking or laughing, and they were definitely not kidding. I just kept thinking that Steve and I needed people like them nearby to help out in an emergency.

Even though Steve left many hours before me, I actually arrived before he did. But that all changed when I decided to take the train from Logan Airport to downtown Boston. If you are ever faced with this prospect, holy cow, just take a cab! I asked people where the Silver Line train was and they pretty much laughed at me and said it's one block up. It wasn't a train but a bus that travels above and under ground at points. Apparently there was a train station started but it was deemed impractical, and now the Silver Line buses use it. You see the stops like on a metro train except you're on a weird underground bus! The biggest issue is that it's really slow, and it stops for a solid five minutes at every stop! It took me well over an hour to get to the hotel, which meant we needed to head off quickly and eat food at Fenway.

My work friend (yes, in Boston) hooked us up at the Marriott Copley, which is walking distance to Fenway, the Copley Metro station (real trains!), and the major Boston attractions. We also had a corner view room with an amenity set-up for us! One funny tidbit was that Steve R. valet-parked his car, which he never took out until we left, for $45 a night. The parking cost him more than the room!

The Friday night game was a ton of fun and unexpectedly not one person said anything confrontational to us directly. They chanted "Yankees suck" a lot, which is strange given the Yankees' history, championships, and general dominance of the Red Sox for the last hundred years, but whatever. In general, the fans were pretty nice to us overall. We were cheering for our team and outside of chanting "beat the traffic" when Rivera came in and Sox fans started to stream out of Fenway, we didn't chant negative things about their beloved Red Sox. Doing that might set someone off after a few beers!

We bought the tickets on StubHub (which didn't exist when we started these trips) and had seats 9 and 12 in the same row. As soon as we arrived, a nice fan said "You must have 9 and 12 because I have 10 and 11"; he moved over without us asking! We had good conversations with the people around us and with the guy in front of us, before he got drunk. His girlfriend was with him and he was honestly more interested in talking with us and ignored her. She was good looking too, with purple underwear. This guy was a typical know-it-all but had some good information on former players and steroids. In the beginning he was rational and would admit that the Red Sox have not had a good shortstop in a LONG time, and we traded our horror stories about AJ Burnett. As he got drunker, he injected himself into more of my conversations with Steve R. He tried to convince us that there are 182 games in a season. We just had to drop it and tell him to Google it when he got home.

Then he thought David Ortiz should get a pass for not running balls out. He didn't understand my point when I explained that players create a bad atmosphere of not hustling, and that not beating out potential double play balls will cost you runs and games—as it did on this night. He thought I was nuts and said, "How do you feel about A-rod gambling?" This didn't have anything to do with our conversation to this point, but my honest answer is that I couldn't care less about A-rod gambling and I hope he gets thrown out of baseball. The Yankees and baseball would be better off.

Then the guy started mouthing off to us about Jeter being a bad hitter and a terrible fielder, and we had to stop talking to him. We used to get upset with Jeter in his last year or two, but even at the time there weren't many shortstops that you would take over him. He's going to the Hall of Fame with 5 World Series rings and he ended up sixth on the all-time hits list. Meanwhile Ortiz grounded out to second in the ninth inning and basically walked directly into the dugout while the ball was still in play. Are you kidding me? You're a DH and can't run down the first base line three or four times a game? A fine role model, sure. Kids, take note. Seriously, anyone doing that should sit down until they are willing to run. I'm obviously not a fan of the Red Sox, but I respect guys they've had like Dustin Pedroia and Kevin Youkilis for their hustle. Big Papi's a tool.

After the game we walked back to the hotel without incident (again, pleasantly surprised by how we were treated) and had fun watching highlights at the bar. Boston loves sports and misery. When they lose, they play the highlights over and over and over again which was enjoyable for us.

Before going out on Saturday morning, I worked out in the hotel gym (awesome). This is not, however, recommended if you will be walking all day—which we do a lot on these trips. This day we walked through Boston Common and along the Freedom Trail, which sounds hokey but it's a great walk past Faneuil Hall, Paul Revere's house, old cemeteries, and the North End. We also booked harbor cruise tickets for the next day. Boston is truly a beautiful city filled with history, and I highly recommend visiting. Would I live there? Never.

For the Saturday game, we decided to try and buy tickets at the game or just watch at a bar. We had bought on StubHub for Friday night at over $100 each, and Sunday night I found a guy from Craig's list for $100 a ticket. This was apparently a good deal as we found people that paid over $200 per ticket for similar seats. On these weekends we normally spend under $150 for all three games, and so we were OK with missing one game because of the ridiculous cost of Yankees-Red Sox games.

Our mindset was: let's offer someone $100 for 2 tickets at game time.

This did not work.

Not even a little bit.

The scalpers were laughing at us when we told what we were willing to spend. Not one of them dropped their price, as there were a lot of people that had the same exact thought as us. The first guy we saw scalping offered us two bleacher tickets for $110 each, which turned out to be the best offer we'd get all day. We also waited on the "same day" sales line that was a mile long, but gave up after about 15 minutes. These are tickets that were turned in—sometimes by the visiting team or, we were told, after someone leaves the stadium the Red Sox re-sell the ticket. It looked like people were getting tickets through this method by the third inning.

After dicking around for an hour, we finally ended up at a gold mine called the Bleacher Bar! This is a true find, and one of the best things we've stumbled on during these trips.

This bar is under the Fenway bleachers, at field level, in dead center field. Inside, there's a garage grate that opens right into center field itself—from the bar, the centerfielder is about sixty feet in front of you. What a way to watch a game! You can't see much going on way off in the distance at home plate, but your view of things going on in the outfield is totally unique. If you watch a game from Fenway on TV, you'll see the big garage doors in center field. When you see it, just remember that behind the one on the right, towards straightaway center, there are a couple hundred drunk fans without tickets drinking and yelling at whoever's playing center.

By the way, it cost nothing to get in! Boston, this was a very unique place and a great experience. The food was good, and they have tables right up against the grate if you want to eat. As you are taking a leak in the men's bathroom, you can see over the urinals and watch the bar and the game while you're doing your business. The only problem with this is that a couple hundred people can also watch you while you whizz. This was a lot of fun! There was one scary scene at the bar with a bottle falling on the cement ground and glass getting into this guy's eye. He was shaken up and obviously not OK. Even though he was a Boston fan, I asked if he was OK and when he didn't respond, I alerted a waitress passing by. She told me not to worry about it and just kept walking! The guy turned out to be OK so maybe she was an MD.

After the Yanks received an ass-kicking on this day, we went out to dinner and then Steve R. wanted to blow $20 on lotto tickets since we saved so much on the game. He thought this was the way people always hit the Lotto. Go to game, can't find tickets, find an awesome bar, buy lotto tickets, we are millionaires. I explained why this was not realistic and the lady at the supermarket selling the tickets backed me up. She said nobody wins and when they do get a few bucks out of it, they spend it right back and more. She said lotto is for losers and gets my vote for favorite stranger met this weekend. I spent $6 and won $6; Steve R. spent $20 and won $4 but he insists that he WON $4.

On a side note, we were eating at California Pizza Kitchen and the waitress asked Steve if he wanted to return his pizza because it was oval and not round. She said people return pizzas all the time for this reason. As far as we could tell she wasn't kidding and I assume these are probably the same people that think it's OK not to run balls out.

When we got back to the hotel, I asked the concierge about jogging to the Charles River a few blocks down (pointing to the river). He looked at me like I had five heads, saying in his Boston accent, "If you go that way, you'll be jogging for a week." What he meant was that I would hit a building and need to make a right and then left to get down to the water. Um, duh? I'm not going to jog through a building. He had that classic Boston patronizing, know-it-all attitude. We did make fun of the little puzzle-piece pin that all the associates were wearing. He said it represented teamwork—piecing them all together—but it was all the same piece! How do you make a puzzle when all the pieces are the same shape and they don't fit together? As ridiculous as this guy and other Bostonians were all weekend, we had fun at their expense.

I didn't go jogging, as Sunday was a rainy day and we headed out on our booked boat cruise to Georges Island in the Harbor. It was only $15 and a cool trip. The only problem was that it started pouring right after we reached the island. We headed back and wound up eating at a place called Cheese Boy—with every type of grilled cheese sandwiches that you could imagine. There are 4 right now in Massachusetts and Connecticut, and this could take off and grow fast!! Mark my words…

Before the game at 8 P.M. (Sunday Night Baseball!) we did a Duck tour of Boston. Duck tours go on land and in the water, giving a nice overview of downtown cities. The driver was of course an old Red Sox fan and was messing with us the entire tour. The back and forth jabbing was fun, but probably ruined the tour for the rest of the people. He did mention that people from Boston are generally stubborn, pig-headed, patronizing, obnoxious, and have a sense of doom. I didn't notice. Steve R. saw this guy in a restaurant bathroom and we talked baseball for a while with him.

At the Sunday night game, our field-level seats on the third base infield, underneath the deck above us, had great views. I have to say, though, that I have *never* experienced a more uncomfortable seat in any stadium we have visited. We were in wooden seats, hard as a rock, with our knees against the seat in front of us and absolutely no arm room. They are by far the narrowest seats I have experienced, including Southwest Airlines. It was probably 95 degrees out and we felt like we were in an oven with sweat pouring off our heads. There's no air movement whatsoever. The rows are like 30 seats wide and EVERYONE needs to stand up to let someone out. You miss a lot of the game because of this and feel bad to go get something to eat or go to the bathroom. At one point, I went to the bathroom and stood behind our section for half an inning. It was like Arctic air blowing on me! If there's a fire, you're dead.

I was online to buy some much needed water when a guy stepped on my shoe from behind me. He said sorry, so I said it's OK, no problem. He then said, "No, it's not OK." Figuring he was kidding, I said, "You're right, it's not OK." He looked at me for about 30 seconds not smiling or laughing and walked away. WTF? My sense of humor and Boston were not mixing well together this weekend!

Note from Steve R.: Josh Beckett pitched that night. He was one of those guys who just seemed scared to let the ball go. He'd wait, and hold the ball, and look in at the catcher, and step off, and reset, and look in at the catcher, and hold the ball, and hold the ball, and the batter would step out, and he'd step off, then they'd reset, and he'd look in at the catcher… Yankees-Sox games are usually four hours plus because of this nonsense. At one point—and Steve is absolutely right about the seats, and the heat, and the claustrophobia, so Beckett's delays seemed interminable and crazy frustrating—so at one point, Beckett's holding the ball and the crowd is just drifting off into a quiet haze, when Steve snapped and screamed out "THROW IT!!!" That got a nice laugh. I hope Beckett heard it.

Steve P. insists he yelled at Jonathan Papelbon, which could be true. Papelbon and former Sox pitcher Clay Buchholz shared the same fear of throwing the ball. In fact, according to FanGraphs studies, the slowest pitchers in terms of "pitcher pace" around this time were Beckett, Buchholz, Papelbon, Daisuke Matsuzaka, and CC Sabathia. This is why those Yankee-Red Sox games took so long!!

And seriously, what are these guys afraid of? Throw the pitch already!

Back to Steve P.:

This game ended horrifically, with Mariano Rivera blowing a ninth inning save and the Red Sox winning in the 10th at 1 A.M. Marco Scutaro got him again, and you could see it coming a mile away. The place was deafening with Red Sox fans whooping it up. Again they did not say a word to us directly, which was surprising and nice. We had more people in our face in St. Louis! They did chant "Rivera's old" which pissed me off but is a true statement. Those 44 saves and 2.11 ERA his final year, at the age of 43, really showed his age. Right on, Sox fans.

I had a flight out at 6 A.M. back to Virginia and took a cab at about 4:45 in the morning to Logan Airport. My plan was to not miss a bit of work, but with about 45 minutes sleep, I had to work at home that Monday. Driving would have been deadly that day. One thing I've learned is to take a day or two from work for these trips, if possible. It's worth it!

Boston was a lot more than I expected, and my perception and reality were completely different. The city was nice, I understand the people a lot better, and would definitely visit again. Could I live there? NO. But I'd recommend it to non-Yankee fans!

Toronto

"That was John Sterling."
"Who?"
"That guy who just walked by. It was John Sterling."
"Are you sure?"
"Positive."
"Let's follow him!"

Thus began the ending to our first night in Toronto. I had recognized the Yankees' great radio announcer as Steve P. and I walked up some steps just outside Rogers Centre. The Yankees had beaten the Blue Jays in the first game of the weekend series, and Steve and I—having had all sorts of difficulties getting to Toronto that day—were wandering around the neighborhood, checking the place out. We hadn't had a chance before the game. That's when we saw Sterling walk down the steps, pass us, and almost get hit by a car.

"THHEEEEEE Car Almost Hit Him!" [say it in your best John Sterling imitation.]

Steve and I both hit weather on our way to Toronto, and the trip was almost the first to get cancelled—despite the fact that all the games could be played in a dome and would go on regardless of what the weather was doing outside! This is actually the downside of having tickets in hand, and a trip planned, well in advance. A massive storm system had settled in over Toronto on Friday morning, and was expected to move slowly east across upstate New York and then the city—exactly my flight path out of LaGuardia, and interfering with Steve's flight from DC, because all the planes were socked in at Toronto and nothing at all was moving. To make it worse, a second giant storm system was parked over New York—Air Canada's friendly reps told me I wouldn't get out of New York until Sunday, and Steve's airline was telling them they were being delayed indefinitely.

This brings up an important point. These trips can't be rescheduled. When Air Canada's friendly rep asked me if he could book me on a flight to Toronto leaving Monday, I told him I was headed up for the Yankees series that weekend—so Monday did me no good. But I had not checked any luggage—this became absolutely crucial, because Air Canada's friendly reps were able somehow to get me on a different flight. Once the weather in Toronto cleared, and after watching dozens of flights get cancelled in and out, me and my carry-on bag were still ready to get on the first flight available. Had I checked a bag into my cancelled flight, who knows what would have happened?

So after sitting for hours in the airport and getting on a different flight, I took off for Toronto with just enough time to maybe, maybe make the game.

Steve P., meanwhile, had been delayed; then seated on a plane and told they'd be waiting on the tarmac for at least an hour; then they got going, got to the runway and squared away for takeoff—when they were sent back to the terminal to wait some more. Their alternative, secondary route—a replacement for the initial DC-to-Toronto flight path—had also been closed. So he waited some more.

He finally got airborne, though, with enough time to maybe, maybe make the game.

We wound up getting to Pearson Airport at about the same time. If you book into Toronto, note that there are two airports—Pearson, which is about a half hour outside the city, and a little airport right in downtown, in the harbor. You can get flights into the little airport, but usually not directly and they seem to cost a lot more. So don't get fooled when planning—we knew it would take us an hour or so to make it into downtown, and it did.

We had several choices—mass transit, which moves you via a busline (The Rocket) to the subway, then into downtown; cabs, which charge by time and mileage; and "limos", which run you into downtown at a flat rate. The choice between the cabs and the limos seems like simple gambling—we took a limo into downtown Friday night when we arrived, figuring that rush-hour traffic and Yankee traffic would slow the trip—a flat rate seemed prudent. On the way out Monday morning, at 6:30 A.M., we gambled with regular taxi—no traffic, fast ride, and we saved a few bucks. Just a few, though—both rides were about $60.

Steve had set us up at the Ritz-Carlton, another great Marriott property, which lies just about a block from Rogers Centre and the CN Tower. The limo took us there, we checked in, dumped our stuff, and made hay for the game. Astonishingly, we walked into the dome just in time to see the game's first pitch to Jeter.

We didn't wander around too much the first night. There's an excellent little "Market" food court on the first base side, along the field level promenade. Great sandwiches, fruit, drinks, etc.—a unique change of pace that gave us a good meal. I can recommend the weird-looking flatbread sandwiches things, which are basically a piece of nice thick bread covered with chili, cheese, sour cream, potatoes, and (in my case) beef brisket. It looks bizarre, but it's delicious. That whole area is a great place to look for food—they have great fries, jerk chicken sandwiches, and other treats.

The Yankees won the first night. The entire weekend the Yankees fielded an array of their B-list players, as the artificial turf and a stream of lefty pitching kept Eric Chavez, Raul Ibanez, Ichiro, and even Cano off the field. Jayson Nix played third, short, and second in the three games, and newly acquired Casey McGehee played regularly and hit a monster home run. He also had a homer taken away by Rajai Davis in left field—more on that later. Fate is stalking John Sterling.

So game goes on, food is eaten, Yanks win. After the game, we toured the inside of the Rogers Centre, formerly Skydome. There's a spot in left field where they do pre- and postgame broadcasts from the promenade. The seats in the outfield are very interesting to try out—we eventually moved out there during Saturday's game. And then there are the dangers of downtown.

We left the dome and decided to wander the surrounding neighborhood, just to get our bearings and look for restaurants and such for the rest of the weekend. That's when Sterling passed us. When Steve suggested we follow him, it seemed to make a lot of sense. I mean, why not? He's walking, for crying out loud—where's he going? Where are the Yankees staying? (Our eternal question.) What does he know about going out in Toronto that we don't?

So he starts to jaywalk. Across a huge street—three lanes in either direction, with pretty steady traffic. And Sterling is not agile—he walked with a surprisingly slow and almost injured gait, as though he may have back or knee problems. (We hope he doesn't.) Anyway, he didn't look like a guy who could Frogger his way across a busy city street. Having waited until most of the traffic was stopped at distant streetlights, he made his move. But he didn't seem to have seen a car that was coming at him, pretty fast. (Of course, maybe he was just trying to get away from us, but we don't think so.)

Anyway, he started to step into the car's path. I think he would've seen the car, but we couldn't take a chance—not with Sterling or with anybody else in that situation, for that matter. So we half-jokingly called out, "Don't do it!" "You'll never make it!" Then he looked back at us as if to say, "You're right! What was I thinking?" I called out, "We love you! Be careful!" He gave us this big goofy grin, and put his hands up to his face like Macauley Culkin in *Home Alone*. It was hilarious. We DO love John Sterling.

Mr. Sterling waited until he had a definitely safe opportunity, and crossed. We followed. At first it looked like he was just crossing the street to go into the Canadian Broadcasting building; we thought he might be visiting friends or colleagues. But then he turned down an alley, which opened up into a concrete urban plaza. We became more intrigued as he crossed into the semi-darkness, figuring that Sterling must know where all the secret hotels and nightlife in Toronto are. We thought he might also lead us to the Yankees. So we followed.

He crossed the plaza and headed for a big, sleek apartment tower. At ground level stood a little iron fence, and a little iron gate, with a discreet little sign indicating some kind of discreet, hidden club or restaurant. Steve and I talked about how this is exactly the kind of place that regulars would know, or players, and that we would never find in a million years if we hadn't followed Sterling.

We watched Sterling go through the gate, through a really beautiful outdoor lounge area complete with fireplace and cushy outdoor furniture, discreetly lit, and into a bar inside. He talked briefly with the bartender—we figured he was telling the bartender that he was being followed by two shady-looking guys—and then he passed through the bar into what looked like a beautiful, high-end private residence. Awesome. We were afraid to go further, so, having seen Mr. Sterling safely home for the night, we decided to figure out where we were and get back to our own hotel.

As we walked away, though, Steve said we should just pop around the corner to the front of the building, just to see what it was. So we walked around, through a commercial alleyway and into the semi-circular driveway that led under the hotel's portico and into a beautiful lobby. It was the Ritz-Carlton! Our own hotel!

This is how stupid we are. While we were following Sterling, thinking he was leading us to little-known Yankee hideaways in a foreign city, he actually just went to our own hotel. We'd been so frazzled getting into Toronto and to the game that we had no sense of direction or location as he led us right back to our own beds for the night. Thanks, John Sterling! We're glad you didn't get hit by a car!

"YOOOUUUUUU GUYS ARE IDIOTS!" [say it in your best John Sterling impression.]

* * *

So that's my main impression of Toronto. Steve P. remembers much more about this trip than I do:

As Steve R. noted, getting to Toronto was pretty difficult with weather delays and possible cancellations. We actually considered cancelling at one point…the HORROR! We've *never* cancelled one of these trips. We also considered driving 400 miles each way, but our significant others convinced us that it was a lot safer to get on the plane rather than drive through torrential downpours for 10+ hours. Plus, airlines are not that great about refunds.

The planes finally took off much later than expected from both NY and DC, and we both said our good-byes to loved ones. I think a part of both us thought this is probably ill-advised and could be the end. I used to be really afraid to fly, but much less now unless flying through hurricane-like conditions. Once my plane got above the clouds it was actually a very smooth flight.

It's always interesting flying by yourself, which could be a common thing for anyone taking these trips and meeting friends who live in other places. (These road trips are a terrific basis for reunions with distant friends!)

Anyway, flying alone, you're usually seated next to someone who either doesn't want to talk at all the entire flight (fine by me), or someone who wants to know everything about you. On this flight, I had a guy up in my business pretty much the entire flight. He wanted to know where I lived, worked, how many kids, what I was reading—everything. Eventually, we both started reading, but after a couple of minutes he looked right at me and declared that he was bored. I mentioned that he still had a lot of book to read, and he replied that he only reads 1 page a day—365 pages a year—which allows him to read about one book a year!

At the time, I thought this was really weird but lately I think this is genius! I try reading before bed and get about 4-5 pages in before falling asleep and usually not comprehending the last few pages I read. Why not just focus on one page a night?

On the plane I was reading my Kindle and decided that this was useless as this guy next to me was not letting up…so I put the Kindle in the seat pouch in front of me and talked with this guy for the balance of the flight. He was a really nice guy who turned out to have plane anxiety and needed conversation. I can relate, so, happy to help. When arriving at the hotel, I realized I left my Kindle on the plane, which I of course blamed immediately on the guy next to me. It can't be my fault…he was the one distracting me and caused me to put the Kindle in a spot I normally would not have! I had previously lost a different Kindle and had just received this one as a gift. I was definitely pissed and wanted it back!! I have never lost anything on a plane before but thought I would call Air Canada to see if they found it. This was a bad idea! I forgot that my cell phone was not set up with a Canadian plan and that airline customer service is a nightmare. I was routed to at least eight different people throughout Air Canada with no resolution but the case remained open for a week. They called me and I called them throughout the entire weekend and in the end, it never turned up! Lesson learned—if you leave something on a plane and it takes off for another city, it's not yours anymore. I spent more on international data/phone charges that weekend than a Kindle PaperWhite costs. Balls!

Toronto is a really nice walkable city with a good amount to do. We did the CN tower…glass floor was not for me but I gutted it out. We went to the Art Gallery of Ontario, the Distillery District for some beers and food, and to their great waterfront with a beach. This particular weekend was cold and it drizzled a lot, which was fine for walking but not for laying on a beach. Not that we would work on our tans…we'd rather grab a bite to eat and watch others do this!

One great Toronto attraction is the Hockey Hall of Fame. Steve and I are from New York and grew up seeing the NY Islanders make five Stanley Cups in a row and win four of them. The rivalry between the Islanders and the Rangers was intense in New York. Chanting "19-40!" to Ranger fans was as popular as chanting "19-18!" to Red Sox fans. The jiving back and forth would pretty much stop when you said "Dude, 1940!" Both teams have won championships in the last few years, which is a real bummer!

One interesting thing about growing up in New York was that you liked either the Mets or Yankees, Islanders or Rangers, but never both. The Ranger fans STILL chant "Potvin Sucks!" after a few quick whistles from the fans *every game*. This goes back to 1979 when Ulf Nilsson of the Rangers was slammed into the boards by Denis Potvin and got his ankle caught underneath him, breaking it and hastening the end of his career. Look, you can still see it on Youtube at https://www.youtube.com/watch?v=74xNCMVtWIo!

Back to the Hockey Hall of Fame. They have a Montreal Canadiens dressing room, really cool goalie masks that have been used over the years, over 1300 hockey pucks on one wall, championship rings, jersey displays, Cup dynasties with information on each team, 3D theatre, broadcast booth, trivia, and a LOT more, including the Stanley Cup with engravings with all the winning team names. There have been some wild rumors of what happens with the Stanley Cup as the players take turns housing it. Some of those rumors involved bodily fluids so we kept our distance but did take pictures.

The interactive part of the museum was great! You can do a shootout against animated life-like famous goalie figures such as Ken Dryden or Henrik Lundqvist. The exhibit measures the trajectory and speed of your shot, which prompts the goalie to respond to make a save. As a teenager I played a lot of street hockey and this was my time to shine! I took a few slapshots that didn't go in and then tried some wrist shots which fared better, but apparently playing hockey is not like riding a bike. To make matters worse there were kids lighting the goalies up and their total scores crushed mine. Kids from Canada know how to play hockey, eh? You can also suit up and play goalie, facing the likenesses of players like Crosby and Ovechkin shooting sponge pucks up to 70 mph. We passed on this one but had a great time watching kids and adults get drilled. It's like playing paintball but you can't fire back.

Before leaving the place we went to the huge gift shop which has a lot of great gifts that really can't be found elsewhere. Steve R.

got a puck that he uses as a paperweight in his office, and a flashing little red GOAL! light on a keychain that sounds a horn when you press a button. I bought a Hockey Hall of Fame Shirt for my son and a unique-looking Toronto winter cap for my daughter. My kids love getting souvenirs from these trips and these were favorites as my in-laws live in Montreal, so they get to show off their heritage.

Despite the weather and the delays, we managed to get into Rogers Centre just in time to see the first pitch to Jeter to start the weekend, like Steve R. said. It's always good to start the weekend off with a win and the Yanks were able to take game one, 10-4. It was 3-2 Yanks in the 7th and they were able to score seven runs in the last two innings. Freddy Garcia started and we were able to see Joba Chamberlain and Clay Rapada in mop-up duty. Joba pitched 1/3 of an inning before getting pulled, which was disappointing as I had my JOBA RULES shirt on. When Joba was a rookie and looking un-hittable the Yankees created the "Joba Rules" to help protect his arm. This made a great t-shirt along with the "GOT MELKY?" Melky Cabrera shirts (I ordered both). Now the Yanks have neither player! Joba had gone from a phenom to essentially un-pitchable, and after just one out Girardi wasn't screwing around even with a huge lead. Bye-bye, Joba.

On Saturday we arrived at the game early to check out different vantage points and see batting practice. Rogers Centre is a huge stadium and you don't want to sit in the upper deck behind either foul line or in the deep reaches of the upper deck. The cheapest seats are on the 500 level. On this level behind home plate, the view is pretty good but can feel pretty far away in the upper parts and down the line is not great. If you are uncomfortable with heights, like me, these are probably not the best seats to select. You get that sick feeling, sensing that if you trip walking down the stairs you're going to plummet to your death. It's great exercise, however, getting to the upper seats!

The Renaissance Hotel is connected to the Rogers Centre, with rooms looking right into the stadium. There have been many stories of exhibitionists, so you may want to bring binoculars to the game! Since we were early, we were able to make our way around the stadium and be right outside the rooms. The guards are pretty vigilant but Steve and I had a good conversation with one guard and he was good enough to let us climb up to view a room by peering in the window from the outside. It's pretty nice…there's a sitting area to watch the game, and there were stairs that led you down to the normal part of the room – bedroom, bathroom, etc. The outfield view is pretty far from the field and you're not in the action of the game. I remember using a luxury box at a football game and it's just not the same for me. There's food, TV monitors, luxury seats, but if I yell at Joe Nathan, I need him to hear me!

The Saturday game was another win for the Yanks, 5-2. Ivan Nova pitched 7 innings with 10K's and little-known Casey McGehee, who the Yanks had just acquired, hit a monstrous home run. I have to hand it to Brian Cashman…he really has a knack for picking up guys that are either underperforming or aren't very well-known, and they produce! Rafael Soriano closed this game as Mariano had torn up his knee while chasing fly balls in Kansas City a month before. Rivera, crying after that game, said he let the team down…Yankee fans know this is nuts but that is the kind of person he is. At 42 there was speculation that this would be the end of his career but of course he came back better than ever the next season! Soriano was interesting to watch…after closing a game he would yank his jersey out of his pants to celebrate. As a Yankee

Fan I loved it, but can see why opposing fans and players would want to sever his spine.

On Sunday we were prepared for a sweep to cap off a great weekend, but after 5 innings the Yanks were down 10-1. Phil Hughes started and really sucked. He was another really promising Yankee that had a lot of ups and downs and never made it to elite status as projected. He has been in the majors for a while with success in Minnesota, though. A few of the Jays' runs came off of an Edwin Encarnacion home run, and it was the first time I noticed the flap down on one side as he rounded the bases. He runs with one arm tucked in and the other in the air and says he is trying to emulate an airplane. I found this infuriating and thought if I were to pitch in this game, I would hit him with my 60 mph fastball then get my ass kicked. It would be worth it!

Just when the Yanks were throwing in the towel—evident by putting Joba Chamberlain and Clay Rapada in to pitch—they picked up 3 in the 6th and 3 in the 7th to get within 10-7. (The talk about Jeter losing range and power, and how he should be moved off of short, were pushing him to another great year. He was hitting .315 in August, and hit a HR and a double to spark both three-run innings.) The bullpen actually held the Blue Jays at 10, but the Yanks could not muster any more runs. And we got to see Rajai Davis make an incredible catch in left field to rob McGehee of another home run. We were sitting down the left-field line, in the middle deck, and had a great view of Davis lining up his jump, timing his rush to the wall, and then launching himself to make the catch. Awesome.

See it here: http://m.mlb.com/tor/video/topic/8877962/ v23840187/nyytor-davis-dazzles-with-leaping-grab-at-the-wall.

Toronto gave us a great series. We were able to come up with two wins *and* a John Sterling sighting which saved his LIFE!

Tampa, Pittsburgh, and Scranton

I am happy to report that almost everyone who lives in Tampa is a gorgeous 19-year-old stripper.

Here's what Steve P. wrote about Tampa—and he's married!

* * *

If strip clubs are your thing, Tampa has one on every corner it seemed like…it was seemingly strip-club heaven. Also, all the waitresses and bartenders give you the impression of being strippers.

On the first day in town we ate at a Greek restaurant in the downtown area, which had awesome food. We were definitely full from dinner and had no intention of getting dessert, but this waitress literally took us by the hand to show us the desserts with a convincing pitch. I don't think it was possible to say no but if we had, who knows what the next ploy would have been to up-sell.

We went to the active nightlife area in Ybor City, with a stop at Coyote Ugly. This is a bar that was all about men getting tortured. Men would pay the women bartenders to whip them, force drinks down their throats, and even rip their underwear lining off, giving the worst wedgy possible. I think that place scarred me for life.

While in this happening area we were reminded why we need to be careful while traveling. A woman was crying and telling us she needed a few bucks for her baby and was leading us toward it. I started to pull my wallet out and then noticed a BIG guy coming from the dark alley and quickly put my wallet back and headed back to the crowded area. He was on the other side of the street but it was an obvious trap to kick our asses and steal our cash.

We went to Tampa thinking it would be cool to see the Yankees during Spring training for a few days. I would be in Florida on vacation with my family, and would take a rental car across from Port St. Lucie while my wife and kids stayed with a friend there. This was a 3-hour drive. Steve R. flew in from New York but the plane had to make a stop for gas along the way. WHAT?

Tampa's public transportation and stadiums do not connect well… honestly the transportation didn't seem to connect to much at all. We stayed at a suburban Residence Inn which worked well having the rental car. My new GPS was great showing us where the restaurants were and getting us back and forth into downtown Tampa and out to Legends Field (now Steinbrenner Stadium).

We actually had tickets to 2 games and one was rained out which didn't spoil things because Tampa was a lot of fun. The stadium is much different than what we expected for a spring training facility. It has capacity for over ten thousand people and was completely sold out, which rivals some MLB teams' regular season attendance.

The biggest problem was that the size and scope of the Yankees in Spring Training brought NO access to the players—which is what spring training is supposed to be all about. The mass amount of security was very annoying. When we first got there and were walking to our seats, I saw Joba Chamberlain warming in the bullpen drinking something. The bullpen was right below the walkway we were on. I yelled down to ask what he was drinking, and he laughed and said it was "JOLT" (remember JOLT?). Before I could ask a follow-up question, security hustled me away. Security was everywhere—guarding all the ramps and doors, and constantly shooing people along who might have stopped for a second to look down at the field. It just wasn't a very friendly environment. It was like they were afraid someone was going to shoot Francisco Cervelli.

The Yanks happened to be playing the Tampa Bay Rays, so of course the Rays had a lot of fans at the park. After we chanted "SHEL-LEY DUN-CAN" before and after the briefly great Duncan had a big at-bat, some TB fans actually told us to shut up. The game ended in a tie which was a bit lame, but it's spring training. The Yankees almost lost but there was an amazing catch by a then-unknown guy named Brett Gardner in CF. We didn't think he had a rat's chance to catch up with a ball lined deep into the right-center field gap, but we didn't know what we were dealing with. He was FAST.

* * *

Steve R. picks up the story:

Tampa was fun, but I'm not sure we would do Spring Training the same way again. Tampa itself is so spread out, and the Yankees are so much the controlling Empire on their own turf, that the nostalgic sense of laid-back, hang-around-the-field-and-talk-to-the-players kind of image we had going down there really came up short.

The Tampa trip wound up as a mash of parts that didn't quite match up. The Yankees' park is a first-rate facility, packed with enthusiastic fans—but traffic in and out was unsupervised chaos, and we had to park on an open field that actually seemed to belong to the Buccaneers' mammoth stadium, across the street from Legends Field. Downtown Tampa was fine, and has a nifty little light-rail to go to Ybor City—but there was little happening downtown, even with the Final Four there that weekend. Ybor City was a fun little historic area, done up nice at night with lights and attractive restaurants and stripper waitresses—but with a bit of an edgy undercurrent, as Steve notes. We saw the de Soto National Beachland, a quiet strip of beautiful sandy beach—which had been the starting point for Hernando de Soto's psychopathic slaughter tour through the Southeast in the 1500s. The Tampa 'burbs were domestic and family-friendly—with strip joints beckoning in every shopping center.

Maybe Tampa and its strippers just needed more commitment from us. I only went down for the weekend, which is a long way to go for two games—only one after the rainout—especially when the plane has to stop in the Carolinas for gas. And Steve's wife and family were just a few hours away, as he jumped over to Tampa in the middle of a family vacation. This provided a good reminder about committing to the trips and trying to leave everything else aside for a few days.

We think a better way to do Spring Training would be to stick to Florida's East Coast, and work our way up through the various camps that are NOT the Empire. Many maps show where these are, and we have hope that we'd get a much better atmosphere. That said, getting tickets might still be tough. We tried to see a game at the Pirates' historic complex in Bradenton, but couldn't get into the park. Seeing the field from the outside, though, was fascinating—it's situated in a regular neighborhood of low-lying, single-family tract homes. For New Yorkers, think of having someone put a minor league baseball stadium in the middle of Levittown. And then picture all of the streets and driveways being used for parking, with families streaming past on the sidewalk to go see the Pirates play the Reds in your backyard. Weird. And definitely worth another trip, to see what the Empire's outposts have to offer.

*   *   *

Speaking of the Pirates, we'll throw in a few notes here on our trips to Pittsburgh and Scranton, PA. From hot weather strippers to coal miners—a natural progression, right?

Anyway, we used to do road trips to Pittsburgh after the Pirates opened beautiful PNC Park. Seriously, this is one of our favorite ballparks—comfortable, great sight lines, marvelous views of the downtown Pittsburgh skyline, and the Pepsi porch showers fans with Pepsi every time a Pirate hits a home run.

We started here because of the park, and also its location. It was about halfway between Michigan and Virginia, meaning Steve and I could both drive there and meet. Pittsburgh has long been an important American city because of its strategic location at the confluence of the Monongahela, Allegheny, and Ohio Rivers. You have to say "confluence," by the way. Steelers fans know why—every game ever played in old Three Rivers Stadium (predecessor to Heinz Field, which showers fans with ketchup every time the Steelers score)—any way, every game ever played there included a broadcaster explaining the origins of the name, "Three Rivers Stadium," and they always said "confluence." Probably the only time that word ever gets used.

PNC is a short walk from downtown Pittsburgh, and it's a lovely walk—across the city's famous bridges, and around a carefully landscaped area that includes PNC, Heinz, and also a number of child-friendly museums. We used to go when Steve P.'s kids were tiny, and he brought the wife once or twice. There's a terrific sports museum in the same area, and also a nice aquarium with a WWII submarine you can walk through. Very cool.

Steve used to book us into the Renaissance in Pittsburgh, which is a simply fabulous hotel. If you ever see a game from PNC on TV, the Renaissance is the big building beyond centerfield with the square cut-out in its middle. It's a classic old hotel, which Marriott refurbished and rebuilt into one of my favorite hotels in the world. It's close to the park, and also walking distance to several theater and nightlife districts downtown.

Also close by is the Pittsburgh Zoo, where we took Steve's kids once. Our Yankee trips someday may include the families, and they may for you, so if you avoid Tampa and go to other places, there will likely be lots of G-rated fun for the whole family between games.

On the other side of Pennsylvania, in Scranton, is the Yankees' AAA complex. The Scranton Yankees are again called the Railriders, and the organization recently re-did the entire complex. Even before the renovations, when we went, this minor league experience was worth doing. The field is very nice, set among the huge rolling hills of the Scranton-Wilkes-Barre area. The team a few years ago had a terrifically inappropriate mascot who used to grind up on children, so you might go to Pittsburgh before you bring the kids to Scranton. But that was a few years ago. That mascot may be in jail by now.

Scranton itself has a tidy little downtown, with restaurants and shopping. There's a sweet shopping mall complex, sweet because it's linked up with a railroad yard with classic old trains at the Steamtown National Historic Site. At the time we went, *The Office* was a big hit on TV, and the mall had signs for the Dunder-Mifflin store. We wandered the mall for an hour looking for it, finally asked, and was told the signs were just a joke. No store. Still funny, though.

Nearby are other museums. We wound up going to the Pennsylvania Anthracite Heritage Museum, and to the Lackawanna Coal Mine Tour next door. The museum was great, but the Mine Tour was even better. Sort of.

The Mine Tour puts you into a caged-in mine car and sends you down into the mines. At the last second before the car started to descend into the earth, Steve P. chickened out and started asking to be let out. You're really caged in, by the way—they lock you into a full cage so your arm doesn't get ripped off on the way down. But you're LOCKED in. Steve's a little claustrophobic.

Anyway, Steve wants OUT. He's worried about his kids, and what'll happen if there's a cave-in while we're down there. So they let him out (I know the mine operators had to be snickering at his cowardice). But his anxiety is catching! It's kind of like someone panicking just before a plane takes off—you start to think, This guy's a lunatic—but what if he knows something? *What if he knows something???* So I ask to get out, too, now frightened of a cave-in! Then when I get out, my brother's girlfriend and future wife Adina wants out! We all got out, the operators laughed at us (they're all veteran miners), and my brother Dave went down into the mine alone. He was the only one with the balls to do it. But if there'd been a cave-in, dammit, WE would've had the last laugh!

In our defense, Steve was worried about his wife and kids. I'd just finished reading *Germinal*, a novel about coal miners in France that features several harrowing descriptions of cave-ins, so that's my excuse. I think Adina's just sensible. Dave's just nuts.

The ballgames in Scranton were terrific. Whether or not you liked *The Office* or want to tempt the Earth to kill you in a cave-in, watching games at the triple-A level is fascinating. You can really see the difference between real major league prospects and career minor leaguers. All weekend we were astounded at how much better Shelley Duncan seemed to be in comparison to everyone else—he was so much bigger, so much faster, and so much a better hitter. He also just played HARD, and he was in the majors a few weeks later. On the pitching side, same thing for Tyler Clippard—he was just BETTER. Duncan wound up having brief bright success and a short career in the majors, and Clippard's been a versatile reliever for a lot of years. You could see it coming, and that's the fun of AAA. The major leaguers down there stand out.

We saw two other players of note. Eric Duncan was a highly touted Yankee prospect, and he played a lot while we were there. He was not impressive that weekend—he just looked awkward and out of place. He was a great football player in college, and he reminded us of when Michael Jordan tried to play baseball—just not the right fit athletically. He never made it as a major leaguer. We also saw major leaguer pitcher Matt Garza, who was coming back from an injury. He blew everyone away, and was almost unhittable. The divide between the majors and AAA is something to see. And Scranton has plenty to keep you busy for a few days—it's a very nice trip to see someone other than the regular Yankees.

Miami

Steve P. continues:

The Yankees against the Marlins was our first mid-week series. Typically my job prevents me from doing leisure trips mid-week, but I had extra PTO time to burn before losing it – "use it or lose it by a certain date", as many of you know. It's typical corporate nonsense but I actually like that it forces me to use all my vacation days each year. It helps keep me sane. And touring a city and watching baseball while others work was pretty cool! I'm also now very involved in coaching my son's 11U travel baseball team, which occupies a lot of my free time, including weekends. The trips also started getting harder to plan once Steve R. moved in with his girlfriend who loves to travel. Christine is very cool and supportive of the trips. She understands how some time apart is very healthy for a relationship. I think this might be a first date question Steve R. asks to see if a second date is necessary.

I flew into Miami from Dulles on Sunday night, and we stayed three nights at the JW Marriott Marquis on Biscayne Bay. The games were on Monday and Tuesday night. I have a good work friend in Miami and she hooked us up! The rooms are really amazing—400 square feet, windows from floor to ceiling overlooking the bay, 42 inch plasma TVs, Bose sound system, and built-in TVs in the mirrors of the bathroom. Originally I thought this was ridiculous but there is something awesome about watching SportsCenter or even CNN as you brush your teeth or shave! I'm not going to spend my kid's college tuition money on this for my bathroom at home, but for a few nights it was nice treat.

The hotel also features a state-of-the-art, full-size basketball court that the Miami Heat practice on (from what we were told). Steve R. can sleep in and I usually cannot, so I typically make use of the exercise room early each morning. This hotel had one that was, of course, pretty dramatic, overlooking the Bay and you could also see in the windows of the luxury condos right next to the hotel. This was interesting to say the least. One morning I was jogging on the treadmill and a couple had left their shades wide open – our glass was tinted but you could see them pretty clearly in bed. He was ready to go, if you know what I mean, and she wanted no part of it – she just wanted to continue sleeping. He must have made about ten attempts before giving up. The guy on the treadmill next to me was laughing and looked over and just said, "Poor bastard must be pretty hard up." It was all too weird, so I moved to another part of the gym! The hotel also has a WholeFoods next door, which was great to get a quick meal anytime. It's no Panera Bread but it did the trick!

The new Marlins stadium was not in the best neighborhood, to our disappointment (and I'm sure many others'), and did not have easy public transportation. It would be great if a metro train would drop you in. There was no real choice but to drive. There was a lot of parking in a massive garage controlled by the Marlins, but the price tag seemed unreasonable at around $30. We looked around and found people selling parking on their front lawns fairly close to the stadium. There was also a Yankee fan walking by who lived in Miami; when we asked him about it, he said it was not a problem, everybody around there did it, and that was all we needed. One woman seemed nice and for $10, why not? She did take our keys and jammed in all the cars (15-20 on a small property). After the game, it was very dark and we had a hard time finding the house (they had no lights). We had to find the owner…this time a guy just handed us the keys and said good luck or get the hell out of here—something like that. It took forever to get off the lawn and getting stabbed was really not out of the question. What the hell is wrong with us? Why are we risking our lives for $20? Principle, that's what! Well, screw principle… the next night we paid $30 and felt really good about it!

We got to see a great pitching duel in game 1—Masahiro Tanaka gave up 2 runs in 7 innings and lost 2-1. Mark Teixeira launched a home run for the only Yankee run and we only mustered 3 hits the entire game.

There was one thing that really pissed us off this game. Matt Capps cheats. He came in to pitch for Miami in the 8th inning, up 2-1 and we were thinking, *Here we go!* But he went on to strike out the side. This guy does a crow hop on every pitch, pushing off the rubber, landing three feet closer to home, pushing off again and then releasing the ball! He throws from what I would say is 55 feet. His back foot is not even close to being attached to the rubber when he releases the ball. Why is this allowed? Steve R. even asked the announcers from Fox (sitting behind the bar in the left field area) before the next game to get an explanation. They said it was something about repeating the same motion every time, which makes it OK; even with men on base. He faced three and struck them all out without a foul ball! He was unhittable! Matt Capps! When we asked Dr. Google later on, we found some stories that Capps's pitching had been ruled illegal in the minors, and that he'd been taken out of a game when the home plate umpire negated every pitch. The (always reliable) Internet said that Major League Baseball had informed its umpires that Capps's delivery was illegal—so why was he pitching against the Yankees? Why wasn't Girardi complaining? Why did Fox's analysts not have a more convincing answer? Very annoying.

The next night Nathan Eovaldi, traded from the Marlins to the Yankees in the previous offseason, had an absolutely disastrous first inning and needed to be replaced after getting only two outs. He had us down 8-0. David Phelps—who the Yanks traded to get Eovaldi—shut us down and the Yanks lost 12-2! As it turned out this game was a wake-up call for the Yanks and Eovaldi. They both went on to finish strong. Sucked we had to be there to see the wake-up call game!

As our blood pressures continued rising during the game, we decided that Matt Capps needed to hear from us since the Yanks were getting their asses kicked and we had nothing better to do. We sat in the first row behind the bullpen in right field. He was sitting in the bullpen with Mike Dunn as the pitchers flicked seeds at each other. We yelled for him to pitch like a major leaguer and not from little league distance. He definitely heard us, as did a lot of fans, so when he turned we screamed "CHEATER!" The Marlins fans had no idea why we were acting like such jerks. It was fun to get this off our chests but we then realized he's doing anything to stay at the MLB level. Sorry, Matt! Please just do this against other teams. He really is something to see.

One other cool thing this game was watching A-rod take batting practice. I'm not a fan but that dude can launch shots! In left field there is the Clevelander Bar right over the fence, then a big wall with a 427' sign on top of it, than a Budweiser sign and a bar area well behind and above this. A-rod hit this bar on a fly, which is a BOMB. He then of course went to the outfield to do stretches and asked each of his teammates if they saw him hit the Budweiser bar. You could see him pointing to the bar as he approached each person. What a tool!

The stadium is pretty cool for an indoor park with a retractable roof. In left field there is glass that stretches from the left field foul pole to center field, so fans can see the downtown skyline! The retractable roof didn't open when we were there, and I asked a few guards and fans why it did not open either night. No rain and it was not crazy hot. We were told that it's usually open, but Steve R. asked Dr. Google this, too, and the (always correct) Internet said the roof was only opened like three or four times all season… hmmm. This was mid-June. This was a great dome but baseball is much nicer outdoors. Let's open it up, Miami! The same thing happened in Toronto. It must cost a bundle to open and close domes.

As with the other cities, we love to explore the city we are visiting and Miami has a lot to offer. One afternoon we went to the Miami Seaquarium, which is definitely a family spot. I think we looked a bit out of place but we are fans of seeing shows with dolphins splashing people, seals going down slides, flamingos, parrots, gators, you name it! I think we were the only two guys together at the park. Screw it—we had a good time. We also stopped at the World Chess Hall of Fame, which is CLOSED! I grew up playing a lot of chess and love the game. This museum building was shaped like a castle but turned out to be a standard business. Too bad—this might have topped the Bowling Hall of Fame in St. Louis for me, or even the Hockey Hall of Fame! We made the trip to South Beach for some lunch and people-watching—very impressive as always. Little Havana was also a very cool place to walk around. I bought an overpriced purse in Little Havana for my daughter, but she loves it because it came from the trip and from Little Havana! Well worth it—always keep the wife and kids at home happy!

I flew back on Wednesday afternoon and took my first Uber (great service) right to my son's baseball practice and back to work the next day. Great time away!!

* * *

Steve R. says of Miami:

Steve P. is right—this was a fun trip. It was a short series, but the city, the hotel, and the stadium were all very interesting and fun. I had gone to Florida a few days before Steve got there—again, it was a midweek series, but I learned my lesson when we did Tampa—Florida is just too far to go for baseball, just to turn right around and come home again after two days.

So with the games on Monday and Tuesday, I headed down the previous Thursday and planned to see St. Augustine and the coast for a few days. This turned out to be a great idea. I rented a car in Miami and drove the three hours up to St. Augustine, an old city that I'd always wanted to see. Steve's Marriott connections set me up at the Marriott Golf World Resort, which is a terrific hotel and also the home of the Golf Hall of Fame. I spent a day looking around the city's historic fort, taking a trolley tour around town, and generally being a good tourist. Afterwards, I drove down the coast to Miami—passing Cape Canaveral, some wonderful historical sites and nature areas, and– to top it all off—Cocoa Beach! Home of Tony Nelson! And Jeannie! They have a little sign honoring this greatest of television shows, right outside a park on *I Dream of Jeannie Lane*! It was a side trip that cost me about three hours, but it was worth it!

Miami itself was terrific. Beyond Seaquarium, which really was a nice, family-friendly throwback (and which honored television classic *Flipper*), we drove out to Key Biscayne and looked at the rich folks' houses. The little commuter rail is fun to take around the city, too, offering some nice views of downtown and the water. Very *Miami Vice*. Who would have thought that there were so many classic TV references to be had in Florida? Or has my focus in Florida just turned away from the strippers? Is it an Atlantic Coast-Gulf Coast thing?

The games were good, too. The stadium has a unique feel to it, which you can sense on TV—the art installation in centerfield that goes berserk when a Marlin hits a home run, the vibrant colors—it's unlike any other stadium. Also unlike any other stadium, they love A-rod there! He didn't play much, being in a National League park with no designated hitter, but he pinch-hit in the first game and the crowd went NUTS! He's still a home-town hero, and now that the Yankees are free of him, we wouldn't be surprised to see him get to 700 homers in the black and red (or orange and black, or white and green, or teal and navy, or whatever they found in the Crayola bin that day) of the Marlins. Plus, Ichiro! And Giancarlo Stanton! They put on a good entertainment down there.

Entertainment is the key. These trips are about baseball, the cities, historic sites, fun people—entertainment. A chance to get away for a few days.

When we started these trips, Steve had a loving and tolerant wife who trusted him to behave while he was away. And she trusted me not to get him in any trouble, either, even though I was single. At this point, I'm also happily married to a loving and trusting wife. Both Nicole and Christine seem happy to get rid of us for a few days every summer, which is awesome, and we appreciate it. They may never let us go back to the fleshfests in Tampa, or whatever it was in Chicago that made us want to stalk Johnny Damon, but we're looking forward to taking these road trips farther afield in coming years. We really haven't done the West Coast or Texas yet, and those are longer, more taxing trips. But Steve's son is old enough to join us now—maybe the next book will tackle the thorny problem of being off to see the Yankees with the whole family!

Acknowledgments

From Steve R.:

Thanks to my lovely wife Christine and to the best puppy in the world, Chloe, for their constant love and support. Thanks also to my mother, Patricia, and my two brothers: famed international photographer Ken Rockwell, and world traveler and raconteur Dave Rockwell. Many thanks to Nicole Pierce and the Pierce family for their support, too. Many, many thanks to my friend Jean-Paul Vest, for the cover design, layout, and production. Finally, thanks to Steve's friends and everyone else at Marriott International!

From Steve P.:

I would like to acknowledge my red hot smoking wife Nicole. She is smart, funny, beautiful, and a GREAT mother to our daughter Rebecca and our son Owen. They are amazing kids and an absolute joy to be around each day….I love you all! Thank you to my mother Ann for her love and tremendous support and my sister Denise and brother Roy. To my Dad who taught me so much about life and introduced me to the great game of baseball….we miss you everyday! I also want to thank Fairfax, VA Adult Softball, which enabled me to meet Steve R. and his brother Dave about 20 years ago!